Be prepared...
To learn...
To succeed...

Get **REA**dy. It all starts here.
REA's preparation for the GHSGT/GHSWT
is **fully aligned** with the Performance Standards
adopted by the Georgia Department of Education.

Visit us online at
www.rea.com

The Best Test Preparation for the

GHSGT

English Language Arts

GHSWT

Writing

Staff of Research & Education Association

Research & Education Association

The Performance Standards in this book were created and implemented by the Georgia State Board of Education. For further information, visit the Board of Education website at *http://public.doe.k12.ga.us.*

Research & Education Association
61 Ethel Road West
Piscataway, New Jersey 08854
E-mail: info@rea.com

**The Best Test Preparation for the
Georgia GHSGT English Language Arts & GHSWT**

Published 2008

Copyright © 2007 by Research & Education Association, Inc.

Printed in the United States of America

Library of Congress Control Number 2006930579

ISBN-13: 978-0-7386-0188-5
ISBN-10: 0-7386-0188-8

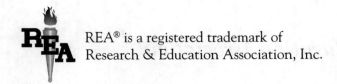

About Research & Education Association

Founded in 1959, Research & Education Association is dedicated to publishing the finest and most effective educational materials—including software, study guides, and test preps—for students in middle school, high school, college, graduate school, and beyond. Today, REA's wide-ranging catalog is a leading resource for teachers, students, and professionals. We invite you to visit us at *www.rea.com* to find out how REA is making the world smarter.

Acknowledgments

We would like to thank REA's Larry B. Kling, Vice President, Editorial, for supervising development; Pam Weston, Vice President, Publishing, for setting the quality standards for production integrity and managing the publication to completion; Christine Reilley, Senior Editor, for project management and preflight editorial review; Diane Goldschmidt, Senior Editor, for post-production quality assurance; Caroline Duffy for copyediting the manuscript; Terry Casey for indexing; Christine Saul, Senior Graphic Artist, for cover design; and Jeff LoBalbo, Senior Graphic Artist, for post-production file mapping.

We also gratefully acknowledge the writers, educators, and editors of REA and Northeast Editing for content development and Matrix Publishing for page design and typesetting.

Contents

About Research & Education Association v

Acknowledgments v

Passing the Georgia High School Graduation Test (GHSGT) and the Georgia High School Writing Test (GHSWT)

About this Book x

About the Test x

How to Use This Book xiv

Format of the GHSGT and GHSWT xiii

Test-Taking Strategies xiv

Section 1: Reading

Chapter 1: Vocabulary and Language, Part 1 1

Passage 1: Excerpt from *Wuthering Heights* 6

Passage 2: Georgia's Right Whales 8

Passage 3: Annabel Lee 10

Passage 4: The Six Nations of the Iroquois 13

Chapter 1 Answers and Explanations 17

Chapter 2: Vocabulary and Language, Part 2 19

Passage 1: The Man He Killed 23

Passage 2: A Superstition Mission 25

Passage 3: Lively Lizards 28

Passage 4: William Shakespeare: Poet and Playwright 31

Chapter 2 Answers and Explanations 34

Chapter 3: Main Idea and Theme 36

Passage 1: Excerpt from "The Yellow Wallpaper" 38

Passage 2: Fuel of the Future 41

Passage 3: Logan's Lesson 43

Passage 4: Tarantula Tamer 47

Chapter 3 Answers and Explanations 50

Chapter 4: Author's Purpose **52**
  Passage 1: Don't Sweat Global Warming 54
  Passage 2: The Hypnotist 57
  Passage 3: The Truth about Year-Round Education 60
  Passage 4: Berrent Art Academy Ad 64
  Chapter 4 Answers and Explanations 66

Chapter 5: Elements of Fiction **68**
  Passage 1: Ripe Figs 71
  Passage 2: "The Thinking Spot" 73
  Passage 3: Excerpt from "The False Gems" 76
  Passage 4: Twins 82
  Chapter 5 Answers and Explanations 88

Chapter 6: Elements of Nonfiction **90**
  Passage 1: Curious Crop Circles 93
  Passage 2: Glorytown Gazette 97
  Passage 3: Safe at Sixteen? Why We Should Raise the
             Legal Driving Age 99
  Passage 4: Daydreams Save the Day 102
  Chapter 6 Answers and Explanations 105

Chapter 7: Poetry **107**
  Passage 1: A London Thoroughfare: 2 A.M. 109
  Passage 2: Excerpt from *Beowulf* 111
  Passage 3: I Wandered Lonely as a Cloud 113
  Passage 4: Ah, Are You Digging on My Grave? 116
  Chapter 7 Answers and Explanations 119

Section 2: Writing

Chapter 8 Composition **121**
  Introduction 122
  GHSWT Writing Prompts 122
  Description of Persuasive Writing on the GHSWT 123
  Developing Your Composition 124
  Content and Organization 124
  Sentence Formation 125

Usage 125

Mechanics 125

How GHSWT Compositions Are Graded 125

Student Writing Checklist for Persuasive Writing 128

Sample GHSWT Writing Prompt 129

Sample Top-Scoring Composition 129

Revising Your Writing.. 130

Revision Practice for the Georgia High School
Graduation Test (GHSGT) 131

Chapter 8 Answers and Explanations 134

GHSGT Practice Test 1 137

GHSWT Practice Test 1 167

Practice Test 1 Answers 171

GHSGT Practice Test 2 181

GHSWT Practice Test 2 211

Practice Test 2 Answers 214

Index.. 223

Image Credits 227

Passing the GHSGT and the GHSWT

About This Book

This book will provide you with an accurate and complete representation of the Georgia High School Graduation Test (GHSGT) in English Language Arts (ELA) and the Georgia High School Writing Test (GHSWT). Inside you will find reviews that are designed to provide you with the information and strategies needed to do well on these tests. Four practice tests (two reading and two writing) are provided, two of which are based on the official GHSGT and two of which are based on the official GHSWT. The practice tests contain every type of question that you can expect to encounter on the GHSGT and GHSWT. Following each test, you will find an answer key with detailed explanations designed to help you completely understand the test material.

About the Test

Who Takes These Tests and What Are They Used For?

The GHSGT is given to all students throughout Georgia who have entered the ninth grade since July 1, 1991. It is given to ensure that graduating students have mastered essential core academic content and skills. The test is given in four content areas: English Language Arts (ELA), Mathematics, Science, and Social Studies.

The GHSWT is also given to high-school students throughout Georgia. It is administered several times a year, beginning in the fall of students' eleventh-grade year. Students will have five opportunities to take the GHSWT before the end of the twelfth grade.

Both the GHSGT and the GHSWT measure achievement in the skills and competencies outlined in the Georgia Performance Standards (GPS). Students must pass each test in order to earn a high school diploma; however, students who do not pass the test the first time are given many retest opportunities to pass the test and graduate in the spring of their twelfth-grade year. Those who fail to pass all of the tests at this point, but have met all of the other requirements necessary for graduation, may be able to obtain a Certificate of Performance or a Special Education Diploma. Students who leave school with either of these documents may retest again as often as necessary to obtain a high school diploma.

Is There a Registration Fee?

No. Because all Georgia public high school students are required to take the GHSGT and GHSWT and pass the tests in order to receive a high school diploma, no fee is required.

When and Where Is the Test Given?

The GHSGT and GHSWT are first administered to Georgia high-school students for the first time in their eleventh-grade year. The GHSWT is first administered in the fall, with retest opportunities in the spring, while the GHSGT is administered in the spring, with retest opportunities in the following fall. Students will have five opportunities to take the GHSGT in each content area and the GHSWT before the end of their twelfth-grade year. Administration opportunities are as follows:

Assessment Opportunities	Writing	Content Areas
Grade 11 fall (September)	First	
Grade 11 spring (March/April)	Retest	First
Grade 11/12 (July)	Retest	Retest
Grade 12 fall (September)	Retest	Retest
Grade 12 winter (November)		Retest
Grade 12 spring (March/April)	Retest	Retest

Test Accommodations and Special Situations

Every effort is made to provide a level playing field for students with disabilities taking the GHSGT and GHSWT and seeking a standard high school diploma. Waivers and variances are made for students who meet certain criteria.

A waiver is a decision by the State Board of Education (SBOE) not to apply all or part of the requirements of the GHSGT or GHSWT to a Georgia student who meets certain basic qualifications, such as

- a disability that makes the student incapable of passing a Section of the test, even with specified testing accommodations, and that student's disability had been documented in an Individual Education Program (IEP).

- a substantial hardship beyond the student's control that has prohibited the student from having a reasonable opportunity to pass a Section of the GHSGT or the GHSWT.

An accommodation is an adjustment that is made to the testing situation based on a disability and identified in a student's IEP. Accommodations may include adjustments in the test setting, the amount of time provided in which to take the test, the way in which the test is administered, or the need for assistive technology.

A variance is a decision by the State Board of Education (SBOE) to modify all or part of the literal requirements for the GHSGT and the GHSWT for students who have

- attempted the relevant Section(s) of the GHSGT or GHSWT four or more times without passing and the most recent attempt is within the last calendar year; and

- successfully completed a structured remedial class(es) after each required attempt to pass the relevant Section(s) of the GHSGHT/GHSWT; and

- passed any three of the graduation tests (four content Sections of the GHSGT); and

- met the attendance and course requirements for graduation defined by the SBOE for the student's graduating class; and

- if the student has a 90 percent or better attendance record, excluding excused absences, while enrolled in grades 9–12; and

- at any time obtained a scaled score that falls within one standard error of measurement (SEM) for passing the relevant Section of the GHSGT or GHSWT; and

- successfully passed each of the End-of-Course Tests (ECOT) related to the Sections of the GHSGT or the GHSWT in which the variance is being sought.

Federal law requires that students with disabilities must participate in statewide assessments such as the GHSGT and the GHSWT. Students seeking a waiver or variance must request consideration for a waiver through their local superintendent. More information on variances and waivers may be obtained at the Georgia Department of Education Web site at *http://www.doe.k12.ga.us*. Students may also ask questions of their school counselors.

Additional Information and Support

Additional resources to help you prepare to take the GHSGT and GHSWT can be found on the Georgia Department of Education Web site at *http://www.doe.k12.ga.us*.

How to Use This Book

What Do I Study First?

Read over the review Sections and the suggestions for test-taking. Studying the review Sections thoroughly will reinforce the basic skills you need to do well on the test. Be sure to take the practice tests to become familiar with the format and procedures involved with taking the actual GHSGT and GHSWT.

When Should I Start Studying?

It is never too early to start studying for the GHSGT. The earlier you begin, the more time you will have to sharpen your skills. Do not procrastinate! Cramming is *not* an effective way to study, since it does not allow you the time needed to learn the test material. The sooner you learn the format of the exam, the more time you will have to familiarize yourself with the exam content.

Format of the GHSGT and GHSWT

Overview of the GHSGT and GHSWT

The GHSGT and GHSWT are designed to test students' ability to read and write, knowledge of basic literary concepts, and familiarity with basic writing strategies. Each GHSGT Reading exam has 50 to 60 multiple choice questions. Each GHSWT has one writing prompt that requires students to write a response no more than two-pages in length to a question.

The types of Passages included on the GHSGT are as follows:

Forms of Information Text	Forms of Literary Text
Subject-area text (e.g., science, history)	Short stories
Magazine and newspaper articles	Literary essays (e.g., critiques, personal narratives)
Diaries	Excerpts
Journals	Poems
Editorials	Historical fiction
Letters	Fables and folk tales
Speeches	Plays
Informational essays	
Biographies and autobiographies	
Primary sources (e.g., Bill of Rights)	
Consumer materials	
Technical documents	
Advertisements	

Test-Taking Strategies

What to Do Before the Test

- Pay attention in class.

- Carefully work through the review Sections of this book. Mark any topics that you find difficult so you can focus on them while studying and get extra help if necessary.

- Take the practice tests and become familiar with the format of the GHSGT and GHSWT. When you are practicing, simulate the conditions under which you will be taking the actual test. Stay calm and pace yourself. After simulating the test only a couple of times, you will feel more confident, and this will boost your chances of doing well.

- If you have difficulty concentrating or taking tests in general, you may have severe test anxiety. Tell your parents, a teacher, a counselor, the school nurse or a school psychologist well in advance of the test. They may be able to suggest some useful strategies to help you feel more relaxed so you can do your best on the test.

What to Do During the Test

- Read all the possible answers. Just because you think you have found the correct response, do not automatically assume that it is the best answer. Read through each answer choice to be sure that you are not making a mistake by jumping to conclusions.

- Use the process of elimination. Go through each answer to a question and eliminate as many of the answer choices as possible. By eliminating two answer choices, you will give yourself a better chance of getting the item correct, because you will have only two other choices to choose from.

- Work quickly and steadily, and avoid focusing on any one question for too long. Taking the practice tests in this book will help you learn to budget your time on the actual test.

- Work on the easiest questions first. If you find yourself working too long on one question, make a mark next to it on your test booklet and continue. After you have answered all the questions you know, go back to the ones you skipped.

- Be sure that the answer oval you are marking corresponds to the number of the question in the test booklet. Because the multiple-choice Sections are graded by machine, marking one wrong answer can throw off your answer key and your score. Be extremely careful.

- Work from the answer choices. You can use a multiple-choice format to your advantage by working backward from the answer choices to answer the question. You may be able to make an educated guess based on eliminating choices that you know do not fit the question.

Chapters	Standards
Chapter 1: Vocabulary, Part 1	**ELAALRL5** **The student understands and acquires new vocabulary and uses it correctly in reading and writing. The student** a. Identifies and correctly uses idioms, cognates, words with literal and figurative meanings, and patterns of word changes that indicate different meanings or functions. b. Uses knowledge of mythology, the Bible, and other works often alluded to in American literature to understand the meanings of new words. c. Uses general dictionaries, specialized dictionaries, thesauruses, or related references as needed to increase learning.
Chapter 2: Vocabulary, Part 2	**ELAALRL1** **The student demonstrates comprehension by identifying evidence (e.g., diction, imagery, point of view, figurative language, symbolism, plot events, and main ideas) in a variety of texts representative of different genres (e.g., poetry, prose [short story, novel, essay, editorial, biography], and drama) and using this evidence as the basis for interpretation.** **ELAALRL1.fiction** The student identifies, analyzes, and applies knowledge of the structures and elements of American fiction and provides evidence from the text to support understanding; the student: a. Locates and analyzes such elements in fiction as language and style, character development, point of view, irony, and structures (e.g., chronological, *in medias res*, flashback, frame narrative, epistolary novel) in works of American fiction from different time periods. d. Analyzes, evaluates, and applies knowledge of the ways authors use techniques and elements in fiction for rhetorical and aesthetic purposes. **ELAALRL1.nonfiction** The student identifies, analyzes, and applies knowledge of the purpose, structure, and elements of nonfiction and/or informational materials and provides evidence from the text to support understanding; the student: b. Analyzes and evaluates the logic and use of evidence in an author's argument. c. Analyzes, evaluates, and applies knowledge of the ways authors use language, style, syntax, and rhetorical strategies for specific purposes in nonfiction works.

Chapters	Standards
	ELAALRL1.poetry The student identifies and analyzes elements of poetry from various periods of American literature and provides evidence from the text to support understanding the student:

	a. Identifies, responds to, and analyzes the effects of diction, tone, mood, syntax, sound, form, figurative language, and structure of poems as these elements relate to meaning.
	  i. sound: alliteration, end rhyme, slant rhyme, internal rhyme, consonance, assonance
	  ii. form: fixed and free, lyric, ballad, sonnet, narrative poem, blank verse
	  iii. figurative language: personification, imagery, metaphor, conceit, simile, metonymy, synecdoche, hyperbole, symbolism, allusion
	b. Analyzes and evaluates the effects of diction and imagery (e.g., controlling images, figurative language, extended metaphor, understatement, hyperbole, irony, paradox, and tone) as they relate to underlying meaning.

Chapter 3: **Main Idea and** **Theme**	**ELAALRL1** The student demonstrates comprehension by identifying evidence (e.g., diction, imagery, point of view, figurative language, symbolism, plot events and main ideas) in a variety of texts representative of different genres (e.g., poetry, prose [short story, novel, essay, editorial, biography], and drama) and using this evidence as the basis for interpretation.
	ELAALRL1.fiction The student identifies, analyzes, and applies knowledge of the structures and elements of American fiction and provides evidence from the text to support understanding; the student:
	c. Relates identified elements in fiction to theme or underlying meaning.
	ELAALRL2 The student identifies, analyzes, and applies knowledge of theme in a work of American literature and provides evidence from the work to support understanding. The student
	a. Applies knowledge of the concept that the theme or meaning of a selection represents a universal view or comment on life or society and provides support from the text for the identified theme.

Chapters	Standards
	b. Evaluates the way an author's choice of words advances the theme or purpose of the work. c. Applies knowledge of the concept that a text can contain more than one theme. d. Analyzes and compares texts that express universal themes characteristic of American literature across time and genre (e.g., American individualism, the American dream, cultural diversity, and tolerance) and provides support from the texts for the identified themes.

Chapter 4: Author's Purpose	**ELAALRL1** **The student demonstrates comprehension by identifying evidence (e.g., diction, imagery, point of view, figurative language, symbolism, plot events and main ideas) in a variety of texts representative of different genres (e.g., poetry, prose [short story, novel, essay, editorial, biography], and drama) and using this evidence as the basis for interpretation.**
	
	ELAALRL1.fiction <u>The student identifies, analyzes, and applies knowledge of the structures and elements of American fiction and provides evidence from the text to support understanding; the student:</u>
	
	   d. Analyzes, evaluates, and applies knowledge of the ways authors use techniques and elements in fiction for rhetorical and aesthetic purposes.
	
	ELAALRL1.nonfiction <u>The student identifies, analyzes, and applies knowledge of the purpose, structure, and elements of nonfiction and/or informational materials and provides evidence from the text to support understanding; the student:</u>
	
	   b. Analyzes and evaluates the logic and use of evidence in an author's argument.
	   c. Analyzes, evaluates, and applies knowledge of the ways authors use language, style, syntax, and rhetorical strategies for specific purposes in nonfiction works.
	
	ELAALRL2 **The student identifies, analyzes, and applies knowledge of theme in a work of American literature and provides evidence from the work to support understanding. The student**
	
	   b. Evaluates the way an author's choice of words advances the theme or purpose of the work.

Chapters	Standards
	ELAALRL4 **The student employs a variety of writing genres to demonstrate a comprehensive grasp of significant ideas in sophisticated literary works. The student composes essays, narratives, poems, or technical documents. The student** a. Demonstrates awareness of an author's use of stylistic devices and an appreciation of the effects created by the devices. b. Analyzes the use of imagery, language, and other particular aspects of a text that contribute to theme or underlying meaning.
Chapter 5: Fiction	**ELAALRL1** **The student demonstrates comprehension by identifying evidence (e.g., diction, imagery, point of view, figurative language, symbolism, plot events and main ideas) in a variety of texts representative of different genres (e.g., poetry, prose [short story, novel, essay, editorial, biography], and drama) and using this evidence as the basis for interpretation.** **ELAALRL1.fiction** The student identifies, analyzes, and applies knowledge of the structures and elements of American fiction and provides evidence from the text to support understanding; the student: a. Locates and analyzes such elements in fiction as language and style, character development, point of view, irony, and structures (e.g., chronological, in medias res, flashback, frame narrative, epistolary novel) in works of American fiction from different time periods. b. Identifies and analyzes patterns of imagery or symbolism. c. Relates identified elements in fiction to theme or underlying meaning. d. Analyzes, evaluates, and applies knowledge of the ways authors use techniques and elements in fiction for rhetorical and aesthetic purposes. e. Analyzes the influence of mythic, traditional, or classical literature on American literature. f. Traces the history of the development of American fiction. **ELAALRL2** **The student identifies, analyzes, and applies knowledge of theme in a work of American literature and provides evidence from the work to support understanding. The student** a. Applies knowledge of the concept that the theme or meaning of a selection represents a universal view or comment on life or society and provides support from the text for the identified theme.

b. Evaluates the way an author's choice of words advances the theme or purpose of the work.

c. Applies knowledge of the concept that a text can contain more than one theme.

d. Analyzes and compares texts that express universal themes characteristic of American literature across time and genre (e.g., American individualism, the American dream, cultural diversity, and tolerance) and provides support from the texts for the identified themes.

ELAALRL3   The student deepens understanding of literary works by relating them to their contemporary context or historical background, as well as to works from other time periods.

The student relates a literary work to primary source documents of its literary period or historical setting; the student:

a. Relates a literary work to the seminal ideas of the time in which it is set or the time of its composition.
   i. Native American literature
   ii. Colonial/Revolutionary/National literature

b. Relates a literary work to the characteristics of the literary time period that it represents.
   i. Romanticism/Transcendentalism
   ii. Realism
   iii. Naturalism
   iv. Modernism (including Harlem Renaissance)
   v. Postmodernism

The student compares and contrasts specific characteristics of different genres as they develop and change over time for different purposes (e.g., personal, meditative Colonial writing vs. public, political documents of the Revolutionary era, or replication of traditional European styles [Bradstreet, Taylor] vs. emerging distinctive American style [Dickinson, Whitman] in poetry).

The student analyzes a variety of works representative of different genres within specific time periods in order to identify types of discourse (e.g., satire, parody, allegory, pastoral) that cross the lines of genre classifications.

Chapters	Standards
Chapter 6: **Nonfiction**	**ELAALRL1** **The student demonstrates comprehension by identifying evidence (e.g., diction, imagery, point of view, figurative language, symbolism, plot events and main ideas) in a variety of texts representative of different genres (e.g., poetry, prose [short story, novel, essay, editorial, biography], and drama) and using this evidence as the basis for interpretation.** **ELAALRL1.nonfiction** <u>The student identifies, analyzes, and applies knowledge of the purpose, structure, and elements of nonfiction and/or informational materials and provides evidence from the text to support understanding; the student:</u> a. Analyzes and explains the structures and elements of nonfiction works of American literature such as letters, journals and diaries, speeches, and essays. b. Analyzes and evaluates the logic and use of evidence in an author's argument. c. Analyzes, evaluates, and applies knowledge of the ways authors use language, style, syntax, and rhetorical strategies for specific purposes in nonfiction works.

Chapter 7:
Poetry
	ELAALRL1 **The student demonstrates comprehension by identifying evidence (e.g., diction, imagery, point of view, figurative language, symbolism, plot events and main ideas) in a variety of texts representative of different genres (e.g., poetry, prose [short story, novel, essay, editorial, biography], and drama) and using this evidence as the basis for interpretation.**
	
	ELAALRL1.poetry <u>The student identifies and analyzes elements of poetry from various periods of American literature and provides evidence from the text to support understanding; the student:</u>
	
	a. Identifies, responds to, and analyzes the effects of diction, tone, mood, syntax, sound, form, figurative language, and structure of poems as these elements relate to meaning.
	  i. sound: alliteration, end rhyme, slant rhyme, internal rhyme, consonance, assonance
	  ii. form: fixed and free, lyric, ballad, sonnet, narrative poem, blank verse
	  iii. figurative language: personification, imagery, metaphor, conceit, simile, metonymy, synecdoche, hyperbole, symbolism, allusion
	
	b. Analyzes and evaluates the effects of diction and imagery (e.g., controlling images, figurative language, extended metaphor, understatement, hyperbole, irony, paradox, and tone) as they relate to underlying meaning.
	c. Traces the historical development of poetic styles and forms in American literature.

Chapters	Standards
Chapter 8: Composition	**ELAALRC3 The student acquires new vocabulary in each content area and uses it correctly. The student** a. Demonstrates an understanding of contextual vocabulary in various subjects. b. Uses content vocabulary in writing and speaking. c. Explores understanding of new words found in subject area texts. **ELAALRC4 The student establishes a context for information acquired by reading across subject areas. The student** a. Explores life experiences related to subject area content. b. Discusses in both writing and speaking how certain words and concepts relate to multiple subjects. c. Determines strategies for finding content and contextual meaning for unfamiliar words or concepts. **ELA11C1 The student demonstrates understanding and control of the rules of the English language, realizing that usage involves the appropriate application of conventions and grammar in both written and spoken formats. The student** a. Demonstrates an understanding of proper English usage and control of grammar, sentence and paragraph structure, diction, and syntax. b. Correctly uses clauses (e.g., main and subordinate), phrases (e.g., gerund, infinitive, and participial), and mechanics of punctuation (e.g., end stops, commas, semicolons, quotations marks, colons, ellipses, hyphens). c. Demonstrates an understanding of sentence construction (e.g., subordination, proper placement of modifiers, parallel structure) and proper English usage (e.g., consistency of verb tenses, agreement).

Chapters	Standards
	ELA11C2 The student demonstrates understanding of manuscript form, realizing that different forms of writing require different formats. The student a. Produces writing that conforms to appropriate manuscript requirements. b. Produces legible work that shows accurate spelling and correct use of the conventions of punctuation and capitalization. c. Reflects appropriate format requirements, including pagination, spacing, and margins, and integration of source material with appropriate citations (e.g., in-text citations, use of direct quotations, paraphrase, and summary, and weaving of source and support materials with writer's own words, etc.). d. Includes formal works cited or bibliography when applicable.

Chapter 1
Vocabulary and Language, Part 1

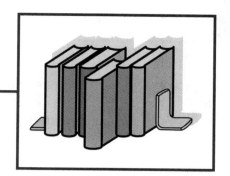

Georgia Performance Standards

ELAALRL5 **The student understands and acquires new vocabulary and uses it correctly in reading and writing. The student**

a. identifies and correctly uses idioms, cognates, words with literal and figurative meanings, and patterns of word changes that indicate different meanings or functions;

b. uses knowledge of mythology, the Bible, and other works often alluded to in American literature to understand the meanings of new words;

c. Uses general dictionaries, specialized dictionaries, thesauruses, or related references as needed to increase learning.

Words with Multiple Meanings

Some questions on the Georgia High School Graduation Test (GHSGT) will ask you about words that have both literal and figurative meanings. You will need to take a close look at patterns that might indicate a change in the word's meaning or function. Some of these words or phrases might be **idioms**, or expressions that are natural to people from a particular area or part of the world. For example, have you ever called someone a "backseat driver"? This is an idiom. It does not mean that the person is really driving from backseat of the car; it means the person is instructing on how to drive as if he or she were actually driving the car. Most people are familiar with this expression.

Cognates are words that have a common origin, meaning they are derived from the same word. For example, consider the Proto-Indo-European word *nekwt*, which refers to the time of day when the sun goes down. In English, this word is *night*. In Scottish, this word is *nicht*.

Night and *nicht* are cognates. While cognates don't always have the same meaning, they often do. On the GHSGT, you can often determine the meaning of a word that is a cognate of a word in the English language simply by analyzing its context.

Context Clues

Some of the vocabulary questions on the GHSGT ask you to define a word used in a passage. You can often figure out a word's meaning by looking at the **context** of the word, meaning the words and sentences around it. Consider this example:

> Kirk was a huge hunk of a dog. When standing upright on his hind legs, he could easily rest his front paws on a man's shoulders. His enormous presence scared most passersby when Kirk strolled in the park on his daily walk on the leash. Other dogs, too, shunned Kirk, fearing death or severe injury should Kirk decide to clamp down on their flesh with his crushing jaws. No one had reason to worry, however. Terrified of squirrels and distrustful of robins and butterflies, Kirk was the most <u>docile</u> dog in the world.

Use the context of this passage to determine the meaning of the word *docile*. Write the meaning of the word on the following line.

_____

Some questions on the GHSGT might also ask you to use your knowledge of world mythology, religious texts, and other works often **alluded** to in American literature to understand the meanings of new words. An **allusion** is a brief reference in a literary work to a person, place, or thing in history, or to another literary work. An allusion can only be understood by those who have read the text or understand the circumstances of the event being alluded to. In this way, allusions can help you understand the meanings of unfamiliar words or phrases. Look at the following example:

> Josh's mood swings were completely <u>erratic</u>. One minute he was sweet and caring, the next he was nasty and cold to everyone around him. It was as if he were turning from Dr. Jekyll into Mr. Hyde.

Even if you have never read *The Strange Case of Dr. Jekyll and Mr. Hyde* by Robert Louis Stevenson, you've probably heard of it. You can use this allusion to help you understand what the word *erratic* means. The characters of Dr. Jekyll and Mr. Hyde represent two extremes, one being kind and decent, while the other is cruel and almost inhuman. These two characters are actually two sides of the same man, and either can take over in an instant. The author of the passage uses the allusion to show how intense and unpredictable Josh's mood swings are. This helps you to understand that *erratic* means *having no fixed course*, or *to be all over the place*. Be aware of references to other famous works, religious figures or symbols, popular myths from around the world, and historical figures. These references can help you figure out the meanings and applications of new words.

Reference Materials

When you can't figure out the meaning of a word by looking at the context in which it is used, or by breaking it down into smaller parts, a reference book is probably needed. A dictionary or glossary can help you to determine the precise meaning of a word. Sometimes, a literary text will include foreign terms. The foreign word or phrase may be included for emphasis, or because the work was originally written in a language other than English. If you cannot figure out the meaning of the foreign term by looking at the context clues, you may want to use a dictionary that can help you to translate the word or phrase into English. You can even look up unfamiliar words or foreign terms on the Internet. Use the technology and other references available to you to help you discover words and find new ways to use words that might already be familiar.

Word Structure

Understanding the meaning of a word's parts can also help you determine its meaning. Many words have some or all of these parts:

- **Prefix:** A prefix is an affix of a word that is added to the beginning of a word to communicate its usage or meaning.

- **Root:** The root of a word is the basis from which a word is derived.

- **Suffix:** A suffix is an affix of a word that is added to the end of a word to communicate its usage or meaning.

If you know the meaning of a word's prefix, root, or suffix, you can often determine the meaning of the word. Consider this example:

I go for a walk each day at lunch. Getting some exercise helps <u>rejuvenate</u> my mind and body.

Rejuvenate most likely means

    A. *keep safe.*

    B. *make fresh.*

    C. *keep healthy.*

    D. *feel relaxed.*

If you know that the prefix *re-* means *again*, it can help you figure out the meaning of *rejuvenate*—to revive or make fresh. Answer choice B is the best answer.

Make flashcards to help you study the word parts in each of the following tables. Knowing the meaning of these word parts will help you answer GHSGT vocabulary questions correctly.

Prefix	Meaning
anti-	against
anthro-	man
arch-	main
auto-	self
bi-	two
bio-	life
circum-	around
de-	not
dis-	not
im-	not
mal-	bad
mis-	not
pre-	before
pro-	for; in favor of
sub-	below
super-	above; better
tele-	far; away
trans-	across
un-	not
uni-	one
via-	by way of

Suffix	Meaning
-able	able to
-er	doer
-ful	full of
-logy	the study of
-ly	like
-ment	state
-ness	state of being
-ous	full of

Passage 1

Read the following selection. Then answer the questions that follow. Use the Tip underneath each question to help you choose the correct answer. When you finish, read the answer explanations at the end of this chapter.

Excerpt from *Wuthering Heights*
by Emily Brontë

YESTERDAY afternoon set in misty and cold. I had half a mind to spend it by my study fire, instead of wading through heath and mud to Wuthering Heights. On coming up from dinner, however, (N.B.—I dine between twelve and one o'clock; the housekeeper, a <u>matronly</u> lady, taken as a <u>fixture</u> along with the house, could not, or would not, comprehend my request that I might be served at five)—on mounting the stairs with this lazy intention, and stepping into the room, I saw a servant-girl on her knees surrounded by brushes and coal-scuttles, and raising an infernal dust as she extinguished the flames with heaps of cinders. This spectacle drove me back immediately; I took my hat, and, after a four-miles' walk, arrived at Heathcliff's garden-gate just in time to escape the first feathery flakes of a snow-shower.

On that bleak hill-top the earth was hard with a black frost, and the air made me shiver through every limb. Being unable to remove the chain, I jumped over, and, running up the flagged causeway bordered with straggling gooseberry-bushes, knocked vainly for admittance, till my knuckles tingled and the dogs howled.

'Wretched inmates!' I ejaculated, mentally, 'you deserve <u>perpetual</u> isolation from your species for your churlish inhospitality. At least, I would not keep my doors barred in the day-time. I don't care—I will get in!'

Questions

1. As used in the passage, <u>matronly</u> **most** nearly means

    A. *scrawny.*

    B. *manly.*

    C. *motherly.*

    D. *muscular.*

> 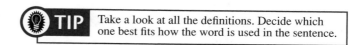 Reread the sentence where the word is located. See if any of the surrounding words or sentences can help you figure out the answer.

2. As used in the passage, <u>fixture</u> **most** nearly means

    A. *a settled date or time for an activity.*

    B. *a person long associated with a place.*

    C. *something permanently attached to a place.*

    D. *the act or process of mending.*

> Take a look at all the definitions. Decide which one best fits how the word is used in the sentence.

3. In the context of the third paragraph, <u>perpetual</u> **most** nearly means

    A. *inclusive.*

    B. *severe.*

    C. *eternal.*

    D. *toilsome.*

> TIP Carefully reread each answer choice to see which would make the most sense in the sentence.

Passage 2

Read the following selection. Then answer the questions that follow. Use the Tip underneath each question to help you choose the correct answer. When you finish, read the answer explanations at the end of this chapter.

Georgia's Right Whales

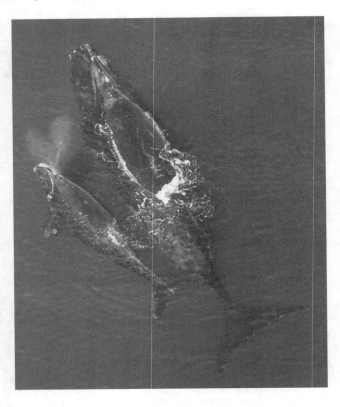

Many people probably know their state's flower or bird, but did you know that some states have adopted marine mammals? Georgia became one such state in 1985, when the northern right whale became the official state marine mammal. This fascinating species uses the Georgia's coastal waters as a calving ground in the spring.

The northern right whale has a large number of calluses—or areas of hard, raised skin—on its huge head. It also lacks a dorsal fin, making it easy to distinguish from other large whales. Adult right whales measure between forty-five and fifty-five feet in length and can weigh more than one hundred tons. Despite their <u>titanic</u> size, these whales survive on a diet that consists mostly of zooplankton and small crustaceans such as krill.

These gentle giants are slow swimmers, which made them easy targets for hunters in the eighteenth and nineteenth centuries. This sad fact actually explains how this species of whales acquired its name. The whales were deemed "right whales" because they were easy to catch, making them the "right" whales to hunt.

Excessive whaling over several centuries caused the number of right whales to dwindle slowly. Though whaling of the species has been outlawed in many countries, people continue to be the right whales' greatest <u>nemesis</u>. With a migratory pattern that flows through some of the busiest ports in the world and a considerable lack of speed, right whales are often killed after being struck by ships unaware of their presence.

Today, there are only about three hundred northern right whales inhabiting the Atlantic Ocean. Fearing that the species will follow in the footsteps of the <u>annihilated</u> dinosaurs, the U.S. government put the right whale under the protection of the Endangered Species Act. Hopefully, a balance of education and conservation will help the right whales increase their numbers and survive for years to come.

Questions

4. According to the passage, the word <u>titanic</u> is used to indicate that right whales are

   A. *obedient.*

   B. *violent.*

   C. *mechanical.*

   D. *enormous.*

   > **TIP** You may recognize an allusion that might lead you to choose the correct answer. However, you can guess the meaning by rereading the words and sentences. Use either technique to come up with the right answer.

5. According to the passage, <u>nemesis</u> **most** nearly means

   A. *associate.*

   B. *sprinter.*

   C. *instructor.*

   D. *adversary.*

   > **TIP** Reread the paragraph. Use other words and sentences to help you figure out the correct answer. Consider what is being said in this paragraph.

6. In the context of the second paragraph, <u>annihilated</u> **most likely** means

   A. *endangered.*

   B. *extinct.*

   C. *exposed.*

   D. *exhibited.*

   > **TIP** Imagine why the author would use the allusion to dinosaurs. How does this help you to figure out the meaning of the vocabulary word?

Passage 3

Read the following selection. Then answer the questions that follow. Use the Tip underneath each question to help you choose the correct answer. When you finish, read the answer explanations at the end of this chapter.

Annabel Lee
by Edgar Allan Poe

It was many and many a year ago,

In a kingdom by the sea,

That a maiden there lived whom you may know

By the name of Annabel Lee;

5   And this maiden she lived with no other thought

Than to love and be loved by me.

I was a child and *she* was a child,

In this kingdom by the sea:

But we loved with a love that was more than love—

10   I and my Annabel Lee;

With a love that the winged seraphs of heaven

<u>Coveted</u> her and me.

And this was the reason that, long ago,

In this kingdom by the sea,

15   A wind blew out of a cloud, chilling

My beautiful Annabel Lee;

So that her highborn kinsmen came

And <u>bore</u> her away from me,

To shut her up in a sepulchre

20   In this kingdom by the sea.

The angels, not half so happy in heaven,

Went envying her and me—

Yes!—that was the reason (as all men know,

In this kingdom by the sea)

25   That the wind came out of the cloud by night,

Chilling and killing my Annabel Lee.

But our love it was stronger by far than the love

Of those who were older than we—

Of many far wiser than we—

30   And neither the angels in heaven above,

Nor the demons down under the sea,

Can ever <u>dissever</u> my soul from the soul

Of the beautiful Annabel Lee.

For the moon never beams without bringing me dreams

35   Of the beautiful Annabel Lee;

And the stars never rise but I see the bright eyes

Of the beautiful Annabel Lee;

And so, all the night-tide, I lie down by the side

Of my darling, my darling, my life and my bride,

40   In her <u>sepulchre</u> there by the sea—

In her tomb by the side of the sea.

⑦ Questions

7. As used in the poem, <u>coveted</u> **most** nearly means

   A. *desired.*

   B. *preferred.*

   C. *rejected.*

   D. *ignored.*

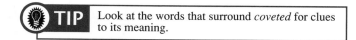

TIP   Look at the words that surround *coveted* for clues to its meaning.

Look at the dictionary entry and answer question 8.

> bore ('bOr) v. **1.** to pierce with a twisting or turning movement of a tool   **2.** to carry away while holding up   **3.** to permit to grow   **4.** to put up with without giving way

8. In the context of the poem, which is the **best** definition of the word <u>bore</u>?

   A. definition 1

   B. definition 2

   C. definition 3

   D. definition 4

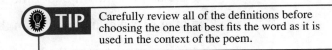
TIP Carefully review all of the definitions before choosing the one that best fits the word as it is used in the context of the poem.

9. In the context of the fifth stanza, <u>dissever</u> **most likely** means

   A. *clear.*

   B. *desert.*

   C. *weaken.*

   D. *separate.*

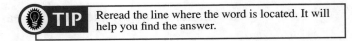
TIP Reread the line where the word is located. It will help you find the answer.

10. As used in the poem, <u>sepulchre</u> **most** nearly means

   A. *grave.*

   B. *ship.*

   C. *castle.*

   D. *yard.*

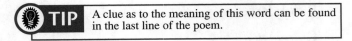
TIP A clue as to the meaning of this word can be found in the last line of the poem.

Passage 4

Read the following selection. Then answer the questions that follow. Use the Tip underneath each question to help you choose the correct answer. When you finish, read the answer explanations at the end of this chapter.

The Six Nations of the Iroquois

Long before the United States of America was created, a group of American Indians known as the Iroquois formed a united government of their own. Their government was known as the "Six Nations of the Iroquois." It was so fair and effective that it helped to inspire the creation of the United States in 1776.

The history of the Iroquois reaches back thousands of years. Since ancient times, many American Indian tribes lived in the lands around New York State. Among these groups were the Mohawk, Seneca, Onondaga, Oneida, and Cayuga. These five groups had been at odds with one another for many years. A mysterious man arrived in their lands with a plan for peace. Representatives of the five tribes met and listened to the words of their <u>eloquent</u> visitor. After that, they decided to make peace and unite into a single government. (Later, a sixth tribe, the Tuscarora, joined the group.)

This government was called the Six Nations, and immediately it proved its worth. The six tribes no longer had to waste time and energy fighting with one another. Instead, they could advance their cultures and defend themselves against common enemies. Between them, the Six Nations controlled much of the land of the northeast. They referred to their shared lands as their Longhouse. They stationed powerful tribes to guard each end of it. By the 1600s, the Six Nations were a force to be reckoned with.

Colonists from Britain and France began gathering in North America. The Iroquois were pressed into making treaties and agreements with them. Although strictly honest in their dealings, the Iroquois understandably felt no deep loyalty to either side. Both sides were frequently unfair and often brutal to the American Indians, and took much of their lands. The Iroquois created a kind of survival technique that involved playing the British and French against one another. By keeping the Europeans' angry with one another, the Iroquois could gain benefits and keep more of their power.

However, the Iroquois could not maintain their "catbird seat" between the European competitors for long. As the British and French began to fight one another, the Iroquois were drawn in and forced to choose sides. Later, during the Revolutionary War, they were again forced to choose. This time, they had to decide whether to join the British or the Americans. The Six Nations became desegregated during these wars. By around 1800, the power of the Iroquois had been broken.

Although the newcomers to the continent, the Americans, claimed control over the land, the Iroquois people never died out. Some of the Iroquois groups that had supported the Americans in the Revolution live today as U.S. citizens. They mostly live on <u>reservations</u> in New York State, Oklahoma, and Wisconsin. Many thousands of other Iroquois people live in Canada today. These people are the descendants of Iroquois who supported the British.

The original lands once owned by the Iroquois are now used by non-Indian citizens. These lands have been changed greatly from their natural state. Today, they are largely covered in highways, railroads, reservoirs, power lines, and other technologies. Ironically, most modern Iroquois reservations have not been given the benefits of such helpful projects. Because of this, the standard of living in Iroquois reservations is usually lower than that in the communities around them.

Despite this, Iroquois reservations are not crude or primitive places. Like most communities, they respect the symbols and customs of their ancestors, but they have not been "left behind" in the past. Most reservations today are fully modernized. Some visitors expect to see ancient shelters like teepees and wigwams still in use. These visitors are surprised to realize that most modern Iroquois live in frame or manufactured housing.

Many reservations are full of small businesses. These include markets, mills, repair shops, and gas stations. The communities also support banks, libraries, sports arenas, museums, cultural centers, and places of worship. Gaming is a major industry among some Indian groups. Tourists from all over the United States visit reservations to try their luck at casinos and bingo halls.

The other major industry, one that provides a link between modern Iroquois and their ancient ancestry, is art. The crafts of the Iroquois are unique and ever more interesting as the world becomes more and more reliant on <u>bland</u> manufactured items. Craftspeople among the American Indians carry on long, proud traditions and skills. They are masters of beadwork, basket and doll making, and pottery.

Much of this art is purchased by tourists, and that helps the economy of the reservations. It also allows Iroquois artists to spread their talents to other communities. Iroquois artwork is also featured in many museums and at cultural festivals. Other forms of art, including music, dancing, and storytelling, are also popular among modern Indians.

Despite the great changes and sufferings among the Iroquois, the Six Nations are still very much alive. Today, Iroquois communities still select chiefs to represent them at the ongoing meetings of the Iroquois Counsel. The Six Nations consider themselves independent and free from the control of the U.S. or Canadian governments. The leaders and citizens of the Six Nations continue to work hard to benefit their people and preserve their customs into the future.

 Questions

11. As used in the passage, <u>eloquent</u> **most** nearly means

    A. *prescriptive.*

    B. *expressive.*

    C. *mystifying.*

    D. *courageous.*

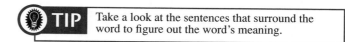
TIP Take a look at the sentences that surround the word to figure out the word's meaning.

12. According to the context, the phrase "catbird seat" means the Iroquois were

    A. in a shifting position.

    B. in a logical position.

    C. in a dangerous position.

    D. in a powerful position.

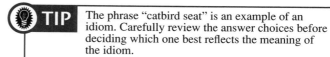
TIP The phrase "catbird seat" is an example of an idiom. Carefully review the answer choices before deciding which one best reflects the meaning of the idiom.

Look at the dictionary entry and answer question 13.

> reservations ("re-zər–'vA–shən) n. **1.** processes or acts of reserving things **2.** limiting qualifications, conditions, or exceptions **3.** tracts of property that are reserved **4.** things that are kept back or withheld

13. In the context of the passage, which is the **best** definition of the word <u>reservations</u>?

   A. definition 1

   B. definition 2

   C. definition 3

   D. definition 4

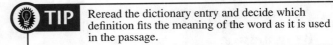 Reread the dictionary entry and decide which definition fits the meaning of the word as it is used in the passage.

14. In the context of the tenth paragraph, <u>bland</u> **most likely** means

   A. *lacking a pleasant manner.*

   B. *lacking definite flavor or taste.*

   C. *lacking distinctive qualities.*

   D. *lacking a tranquil quality.*

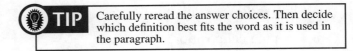 Carefully reread the answer choices. Then decide which definition best fits the word as it is used in the paragraph.

✔ Answers

1. C

   The word *matronly* is used here to mean *motherly*. The housekeeper has a strict set of rules that the speaker cannot seem to break, much in the way that many mothers in the nineteenth century did in order to keep a household running smoothly. Despite the speaker's best efforts, he cannot get the housekeeper to budge on her schedule.

2. B

   Here the author is using the word *fixture* to describe someone that has been long associated with a place. The housekeeper has been there so long that she is viewed almost as a part of the house.

3. C

   The speaker uses this word to illustrate his hope that the inmates will experience everlasting isolation from others for being so unwelcoming to him. This will ensure that the inmates will be forever lonely without the company of others.

4. D

   The author may be alluding to the huge ocean liner the *Titanic* in order to help you understand just how enormous right whales actually are.

5. D

   A *nemesis* is someone who is an enemy or adversary of another person or thing. In this case, the right whale's greatest nemesis is mankind. The passage tells you that humans are often responsible for right whale deaths because shipping routes fall into the animals' natural migratory path.

6. B

   The author alludes to the long-gone dinosaurs to show the reader that the word annihilated means extinct. Efforts by several organizations and the federal government are helping keep the right whales from becoming extinct like the dinosaurs.

7. A

   The speaker and Annabel Lee have a love that is more than love. This is a love so great that even the angels in heaven envy the couple. The angels wanted or desired a love like this, and because they couldn't have it, they took it away from the speaker and Annabel Lee by separating them.

8. B

As it is used in the poem, *bore* means *to carry away while holding up*. The speaker says that this is what Annabel Lee's kinsmen did. The other definitions do not fit the word as it is used in the context of the poem.

9. D

By looking at the words that surround the word *dissever*, you can see that the word means *to separate*. The speaker is saying that despite the fact that Annabel Lee has died, their love is one that is so strong that their souls will never be separated.

10. A

The last line of the poem says, "In her tomb by the side of the sea." A tomb is a place where people are buried. The speaker is referring to Annabel Lee's grave by the side of the sea.

11. B

As used in the passage, *eloquent*—consistent with its dictionary definition—means *marked by forceful or fluent expression*. This eloquent visitor used expressive words to convince the tribes to come to unite as one.

12. D

By looking at the sentences that surround the idiom "catbird seat," you can see that the phrase means that the Iroquois gained benefits and power by playing the English and the French against one another. The phrase was first seen in print in a short story of the same name by James Thurber in 1942 and has come to mean that a person is in an advantageous position. The origins of the idiom are unknown.

13. C

Many Iroquois now live on reservations set aside by the government. The other definitions correctly define the word *reservations*, but only answer choice C fits the meaning of the word as it is used by the author in this passage.

14. C

The word *bland* can be used in a variety of ways. In this sentence, it is important to look at the context to decide which answer choice is best. All of the definitions are correct according to the dictionary; however, only answer choice C provides the definition of the word as it is used in the sentence.

Chapter 2

Vocabulary and Language, Part 2

Georgia Performance Standards

ELAALRL1 The student demonstrates comprehension by identifying evidence (e.g., diction, imagery, point of view, figurative language, symbolism, plot events, and main ideas) in a variety of texts representative of different genres (e.g., poetry, prose [short story, novel, essay, editorial, biography], and drama) and using this evidence as the basis for interpretation.

ELAALRL1.fiction. The student identifies, analyzes, and applies knowledge of the structures and elements of American fiction and provides evidence from the text to support understanding; the student

    a. locates and analyzes such elements in fiction as language and style, character development, point of view, irony, and structures (e.g., chronological, in medias res, flashback, frame narrative, epistolary novel) in works of American fiction from different time periods;

    d. analyzes, evaluates, and applies knowledge of the ways authors use techniques and elements in fiction for rhetorical and aesthetic purposes.

ELAALRL1.nonfiction. The student identifies, analyzes, and applies knowledge of the purpose, structure, and elements of nonfiction and/or informational materials and provides evidence from the text to support understanding; the student

    b. analyzes and evaluates the logic and use of evidence in an author's argument;

    c. analyzes, evaluates, and applies knowledge of the ways authors use language, style, syntax, and rhetorical strategies for specific purposes in nonfiction works.

ELAALRL1.poetry. The student identifies and analyzes elements of poetry from various periods of American literature and provides evidence from the text to support understanding; the student

   a. identifies, responds to, and analyzes the effects of diction, tone, mood, syntax, sound, form, figurative language, and structure of poems as these elements relate to meaning:

      i. **Sound:** alliteration, end rhyme, slant rhyme, internal rhyme, consonance, assonance

      ii. **Form:** fixed and free, lyric, ballad, sonnet, narrative poem, blank verse

      iii. **Figurative language:** personification, imagery, metaphor, conceit, simile, metonymy, synecdoche, hyperbole, symbolism, allusion

   b. analyzes and evaluates the effects of diction and imagery (e.g., controlling images, figurative language, extended metaphor, understatement, hyperbole, irony, paradox, and tone) as they relate to underlying meaning.

Author's Word Choice

In Chapter 1, you learned how to identify the meanings of unfamiliar vocabulary words—as well as idioms and words with multiple meanings—by using context clues. However, other questions on the Georgia High School Graduation Test (GHSGT) will test your understanding of vocabulary in a different way. These questions will ask you to analyze why authors use specific words or phrases in a selection. You will see throughout the book many of the questions in this lesson as they apply to the different genres of writing.

When an author writes, he or she must make hundreds of decisions about words, phrases, and sentences for both **rhetorical** (relating to the creation of effective writing or speech) and **aesthetic** (relating to a beautiful appearance) reasons. Simply put, writers want their work to sound and look good to readers.

Choosing the right language to use in the right situation to achieve maximum effectiveness is called diction. Read these examples:

   1. "Good afternoon. How are you doing today, Grandma?" asked Rose.

   2. "Yo, Gram, what's up?" hollered Rose.

Essentially, these two sentences say the same thing. However, the diction the author chooses to use will determine whether readers perceive Rose as respectful (1) or disrespectful (2) to her grandmother.

Choosing how to put words together to make effective clauses and sentences is called **syntax**. When an author writes, he or she chooses words carefully in order to convey a specific message to his or her readers. An author tries to use words that accurately describe tastes, sounds, sights, smells, or feelings. By using words that appeal to readers' senses, an author can create vivid images in the minds of readers. Each time an author makes a deliberate word choice, it is meant not only to support the theme of the work, but also to communicate his or her point of view or purpose for writing. On the GHSGT, you might be asked what the point of view in a story reveals about the narrator or another character in the story. Some of the questions on the GHSGT, especially questions about poems, will ask you to determine the meaning of figurative language and literary devices such as similes, metaphors, symbols, and personification. Others might ask you to describe the structure of a passage. For example, does the author present a problem followed by a solution or list a series of events in chronological order? Is the poem written in lyric, ballad, or narrative form? Some questions may ask you to determine how an author's depiction of a character helps to develop that character's personality or attitude (as demonstrated in the example above).

Tone and Mood

Other questions on the GHSGT will ask you about the tone or the mood of the story. The **tone** reflects the author's attitude about what he or she is writing about. If an author is writing about a happy childhood memory, his or her tone might be whimsical or sentimental. If an author is writing a first-person story about a character who is upset, the tone might be angry or sarcastic. The **mood** of a piece of writing is the feeling the writing evokes in the reader. The mood might be mysterious, suspenseful, or sentimental. The following table gives some common words that are used to describe tone and mood.

Common Words Used to Describe Tone and Mood			
ambivalent	encouraging	inspirational	remorseful
amused	enthusiastic	ironic	rude
angry	envious	judgmental	sad
anxious	excited	lighthearted	sarcastic
appreciative	fearful	malicious	sentimental
bewildered	formal	mischievous	serious
bitter	friendly	mysterious	sincere
bored	frustrated	nervous	snobbish

calm	gentle	neutral	suspenseful
cheerful	gloomy	nostalgic	sympathetic
concerned	honest	objective	tense
critical	hopeful	pensive	thankful
curious	humorous	pessimistic	tolerant
defensive	imaginative	proud	tragic
depressed	impersonal	reflective	vindictive
determined	indifferent	relaxed	whimsical
dissatisfied	innocent	relieved	worrisome

Passage 1

Read the following selection. Then answer the questions that follow. Use the Tip underneath each question to help you choose the correct answer. When you finish, read the answer explanations at the end of this chapter.

The Man He Killed

by Thomas Hardy

"Had he and I but met

By some old ancient inn,

We should have sat us down to wet

Right many a nipperkin![1]

5   "But ranged as infantry,

And staring face to face,

I shot at him and he at me,

And killed him in his place.

"I shot him dead because—

10   Because he was my foe,

Just so; my foe of course he was;

That's clear enough; although

"He thought he'd 'list perhaps,

Off-hand, like—just as I—

15   Was out of work—had sold his traps[2]—

No other reason why.

"Yes, quaint and curious war is!

You shoot a fellow down

You'd treat if met where any bar is,

20   Or help to half-a-crown."

—1902

[1]cup

[2]his personal things

❓ Questions

1. In the poem, Hardy repeats the word *foe* in order to

   A. emphasize that the narrator and the man were long-time enemies.

   B. suggest that the narrator has no regrets about killing the man.

   C. emphasize that the narrator is trying to justify killing the man.

   D. suggest that the man could just as easily have killed the narrator.

    Read the whole stanza containing lines 10 and 11, and pay close attention to how the stanza ends. How does the narrator seem to feel about calling the other man a "foe"?

2. The point of view used in the passage reveals

   A. the narrator's indifference toward killing a man in the war.

   B. the narrator's sarcasm and criticism of the war.

   C. the narrator's fear of fighting in another war.

   D. the narrator's remorse over the destruction the war caused.

    The narrator describes the war as "quaint and curious." How are these words different from the words most people would use to describe war? Why do you think the narrator chose to describe war this way?

3. The author depicts the narrator and the man he killed in the war sitting at an inn together in order to show war's

   A. opportunity.

   B. efficiency.

   C. treachery.

   D. absurdity.

    Read the first two stanzas of the poem again. How would the narrator and the man he killed have acted under normal circumstances? Then consider why the narrator considered the man an enemy.

Passage 2

Read the following selection. Then answer the questions that follow. Use the Tip underneath each question to help you choose the correct answer. When you finish, read the answer explanations at the end of this chapter.

A Superstition Mission

"The exam will be on Monday," announced Mrs. Keenan, the science teacher. "You'll have the entire weekend, so there will be no excuse for forgetting to prepare!"

Pete squirmed in his seat, his mind racing with considerations of all of the tasks he'd need to perform before the exam. The exam would cover the first five chapters in their massive textbook—chapters that covered topics ranging from earth science to space exploration. He found the material difficult and knew he'd have to really make an effort in order to get a decent grade.

Mentally reviewing his schedule for the weekend, Pete knew right away he'd need to dedicate most of his time over the next few days to preparing for Mrs. Keenan's test. He was going to start preparing immediately after school, but he remembered that it was Friday the thirteenth. Not wanting to jinx himself, Pete instead resolved to start preparing bright and early on Saturday morning. On Friday night, he placed his textbook on the head of his bed, and stacked next to it a pile of science handout sheets.

"Here's everything I need to absorb by Monday afternoon," he thought, plopping a pillow on top of it all. "So I'll start by sleeping on it so maybe the information will soak up into my brain."

Pete rested his tired head on the pillow. Though the pillow was lumpy from all the papers underneath, Pete knew his discomfort was necessary. He didn't want a single thing to go wrong with his preparation routine.

Pete woke up at nine o'clock on Saturday, since nine was his lucky number. He'd spent the night dreaming, wading in the deluge of science topics he needed to master by Monday. He realized now more than ever that he needed some special preparations. For breakfast, he ate some cereal with marshmallows shaped like traditional good-luck charms like horseshoes and four-leaf clovers. "This'll fill me up with good luck," he thought as he scanned through the topics of his textbook.

Each time he saw a new chapter heading in his book, he thought of an appropriate activity to help him absorb its information. For the chapter on the revolutions of planets, he spun his textbook around three times—three was his personal lucky number. Then he spun his chair around, too, for good measure. When he saw information about the winds that blew across Earth, he remembered a good-luck ritual of blowing on his hands.

"Maybe that'll help my hands write down the correct answers on Monday," Pete thought hopefully.

Again, he slept with the textbook and handouts under his pillow, and all day Sunday he observed every superstitious ritual he could think of. He didn't step on any cracks in the sidewalk, he entered and exited his house through the same door, and he kept well away from any roving black cats. Then, on Sunday night, Pete carefully chose his lucky sweatshirt, his lucky socks, and his lucky baseball cap. He even accessorized with a lucky charm that his grandmother had given him years ago.

Pete was feeling confident as he swaggered into class, feeling assured that his weekend of preparation would pay off. Mrs. Keenan passed out the exams and Pete grabbed his enthusiastically, gripping his old, chewed-up lucky pencil.

The next day, Pete found out that he'd failed the test. He shook his head in amazement. "I did everything I could to prepare," he said. "Who'd have thought I'd forget to read the book?"

⑦ Questions

4. The use of the different superstitions in the poem helps to create a tone that is

   A. whimsical.

   B. inspirational.

   C. pessimistic.

   D. dissatisfied.

 TIP | Think about the different superstitions Pete has in the story: recalling his lucky numbers, blowing on his hands, using a lucky pencil, etc. At the end of the story, we learn that Pete's superstitions didn't help him at all. How does this make his superstitions seem?

5. The author depicts Pete swaggering into class on the day of the test in order to show Pete's

   A. embarrassment.

   B. confidence.

   C. nervousness.

   D. astonishment.

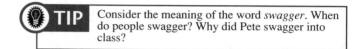

TIP   Consider the meaning of the word *swagger*. When do people swagger? Why did Pete swagger into class?

6. The author described Pete's sleep experience saying,

   He'd spent the night dreaming, wading in the deluge of science topics he needed to master by Monday.

   The **most likely** reason the author chose these words would be to

   A. show that Pete was thinking about the many things he needed to study.

   B. imply that Pete was overwhelmed by all that he had to learn for the test.

   C. indicate that Pete thought his teacher had assigned too much homework.

   D. demonstrate that Pete had a good grasp on many different science topics.

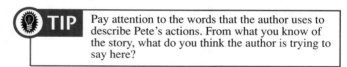

TIP   Pay attention to the words that the author uses to describe Pete's actions. From what you know of the story, what do you think the author is trying to say here?

Passage 3

Read the following selection. Then answer the questions that follow. Use the Tip underneath each question to help you choose the correct answer. When you finish, read the answer explanations at the end of this chapter.

Lively Lizards

The Colorful Chameleon

Standing in the window of the local pet shop, you carefully examine a lizard as he expertly maneuvers along the length of a slim branch, like a tightrope walker at the circus. Having found a comfortable place beneath the warmth of a light bulb, the lizard settles in for a nap. You watch the strange-looking creature for a few more minutes, and just as you're about to walk away, the lizard's bright green skin turns white right before your eyes! Intrigued by the spectacle you've just witnessed, you enter the pet store to learn more about this magnificent magician.

Land of Lizards

Wild chameleons live in very few places in the world. Those that are housed as pets in the United States and other places on the continent were shipped from Madagascar, India, Yemen, Kenya, or South Africa. About half of the world's chameleon population, which totals about 135 different species, can be found in Madagascar, an island off the coast of Africa. In fact, 59 of the world's chameleon species can be found only in Madagascar, including the largest species, the Parson's Chameleon, which can grow to be the size of a cat.

Amazing Abilities

Chameleons are known for their ability to change the color of their skin. Most people believe that chameleons change color to blend in with their surroundings; however, this is a widespread misconception about these lizards. Chameleons change color according to temperature or mood, or to communicate with other chameleons. They do not have an unlimited array of colors, but they can exhibit shades of green, brown, red, blue, yellow, white, or black skin. Despite the fact that many normally appear to be green or brown, the outer layer of a chameleon's skin is actually transparent. It is the layers of skin cells underneath that contain pigments called chromatophores and melanin.

These cells can expand and contract depending on a chameleon's body temperature or mood. If a chameleon is too warm, its brain will tell the lighter-colored skin cells to enlarge so that it can reflect light off of its body rather than absorbing it. Bright colors are used to attract mates, and dark colors are used to show enemies that the chameleon is ready to attack, if necessary. In self-defense, a chameleon might also hiss and spring at its would-be attacker.

Human Threat

Snakes and birds must be avoided because they can eat chameleons, but the greatest threat to chameleons by far is the human race. When trees are cut down to create farmlands, fuel for heat, or housing materials, the arboreal chameleon has nowhere to live and must seek out a new habitat. Some chameleons adapt well to these changes and successfully discover new dwellings. Others don't fare as well. Agricultural chemicals can also kill off these likable creatures. Another—perhaps greater—threat to chameleon populations is their export for sale in America and other countries. Almost 100,000 chameleons are shipped out of their countries of origin every year. Some are not equipped to survive the transport, and others will not adapt to the North American climate. The ones that do survive the trip are then sold in pet stores and on the Internet. Many countries are working to pass laws banning chameleon export, so that chameleons can live and thrive on their native lands.

(?) Questions

7. In this situation, the author's purpose is primarily to

   A. entertain.

   B. instruct.

   C. inform.

   D. persuade.

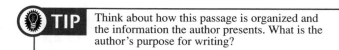

TIP | Think about how this passage is organized and the information the author presents. What is the author's purpose for writing?

8. Which **best** describes the way in which the passage is structured?

    A. a series of events given in order

    B. a main idea and supporting details

    C. a problem and various solutions

    D. an argument and counterarguments

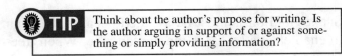

TIP   Think about the author's purpose for writing. Is the author arguing in support of or against something or simply providing information?

9. The phrase "like a tightrope walker at the circus" is a simile for the chameleon's

    A. amazing color changes.

    B. need for a warm habitat.

    C. interesting appearance.

    D. agility while climbing.

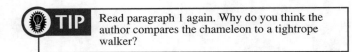

TIP   Read paragraph 1 again. Why do you think the author compares the chameleon to a tightrope walker?

10. As used to describe the chameleon in the pet shop window, the phrase "magnificent magician" is an example of which literary device?

    A. irony

    B. allusion

    C. synecdoche

    D. personification

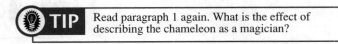

TIP   Read paragraph 1 again. What is the effect of describing the chameleon as a magician?

Passage 4

Read the following passage. Then answer the questions that follow. Use the Tip underneath each question to help you choose the correct answer. When you finish, read the answer explanations at the end of this chapter.

William Shakespeare: Poet and Playwright

From the finest universities, to countless bedside tables and even the pages of the Internet, the words of William Shakespeare can be found in all four corners of the world. Shakespeare is, arguably, the most famous and one of the most well-respected writers in the history of the English language. The writer's plays and poems have been translated into every current living language. Centuries after his death, Shakespeare's works are still examined by scholars, his words recited by lovers, and his life and times explored by historians. However, despite being one of the most widely recognized figures in modern history, very little is known about the mysterious writer.

It is believed that William Shakespeare was born on April 23, 1564, in Stratford-upon-Avon, though there is no clear documentation verifying this date. Historical evidence shows that Shakespeare was baptized on April 26, and many believe that his birth occurred three days prior. Shakespeare's father, John Shakespeare, was variously employed, eventually taking on a position as town official. His mother, Mary, inherited a great deal of property after the death of her father, allowing the Shakespeare family to live comfortably for some time, though they experienced a number of financial problems in later years. Shakespeare was lucky to have survived into adulthood. Several of his siblings died before they reached their teens, some succumbing to the plague and others dying from other common childhood ailments.

It is believed that Shakespeare attended the local public school, possibly ending at the high school level, but there is little documentation to support this idea. It is known that Shakespeare, at the age of eighteen, married twenty-six-year-old Anne Hathaway. The couple moved to London where they raised three children. After this, historians note a gap of about seven years where the activities of the Bard are largely unknown. The next mention of Shakespeare is by Robert Green, a playwright who offered the young writer his first taste of negative criticism in 1592. How and why Shakespeare became involved in the theater is unknown. He seems to have started out as an actor and then had his own plays published. Shakespeare joined the acting troupe the Lord Chamberlain's Men, which would later be renamed the King's Men, after the death of Queen Elizabeth. In this group, Shakespeare sharpened his skills as both an actor and a writer.

It is thought that the plays *Two Gentlemen of Verona* and *Love's Labour's Lost* were written during this early period in Shakespeare's career. He would go on to write such well-known works as *Romeo and Juliet*, *Hamlet*, *Othello*, and many others. Of course, besides being a marvelous playwright, Shakespeare authored over a hundred sonnets, many of which are still regarded as literary masterpieces. Eventually, Shakespeare would open the now-famous Globe Theatre in London. Here, the King's Men performed many of the Bard's plays to excited audience members.

It is believed that Shakespeare retired from the stage in 1613. The date of his death is, ironically, thought to be April 23, 1616. Shakespeare's works continue to enchant readers everywhere. His stories have a universal quality that has transcended time and space, making Shakespeare literature's most famous and grandest figure.

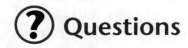 Questions

11. The author described Shakespeare saying,

    William Shakespeare can be found in all four corners of the world.

    The **most likely** reason the author chose these words would be to

    A. imply that Shakespeare's works have been set in cities around the world.

    B. indicate that Shakespeare's works are stored in four different areas.

    C. show that Shakespeare's works have been published all over the world.

    D. reveal that Shakespeare's works are based on his own world travels.

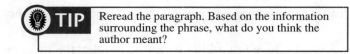

TIP Reread the paragraph. Based on the information surrounding the phrase, what do you think the author meant?

12. Which **best** describes the way in which the passage is structured?

    A. a main idea with anecdotes

    B. chronological order

    C. comparison and contrast

    D. a conflict followed by the resolution

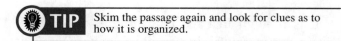

TIP Skim the passage again and look for clues as to how it is organized.

13. The phrase "sharpened his skills" is a metaphor for Shakespeare

   A. teaching others how to write.

   B. practicing writing until he got better.

   C. finding out that he was not a good writer.

   D. receiving bad reviews of his writings.

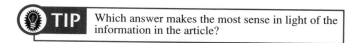 Which answer makes the most sense in light of the information in the article?

14. The way the author uses language in the passage reveals

   A. the uncertainty that surrounds Shakespeare's life.

   B. the inspiration people draw from Shakespeare's work.

   C. Shakespeare's unfortunate childhood.

   D. Shakespeare's determination to succeed.

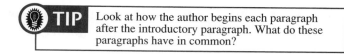 Look at how the author begins each paragraph after the introductory paragraph. What do these paragraphs have in common?

✔ Answers

1. **C**

    The narrator doesn't seem convinced that the man was a "foe," and so Hardy repeats the word *foe* to show that the narrator is trying to justify the killing.

2. **B**

    The narrator uses the words "quaint and curious" to be sarcastic because he doesn't really approve of war and feels guilty that he had to kill a man during a war.

3. **D**

    The author wants readers to see the absurdity of war by showing that under normal circumstances, the narrator and the man he killed probably would have been friends, but because they were fighting on opposite sides of a war, they were enemies sent to kill each other.

4. **A**

    At the end of the story, we learn that Pete's superstitions had no effect on how well he performed on the test, which makes them all seem silly or quirky. Therefore, the best word to describe the tone of the story is *whimsical*.

5. **B**

    To *swagger* means *to strut with pride or self-assurance*. Pete felt certain that by following all of his superstitions, he would get a good grade on his test. Therefore, the author depicts him swaggering into class to show that he felt confident that he would do well.

6. **A**

    To be caught in a deluge means that one can't stay afloat, but Pete is not overwhelmed. He seems confident that he'll do well. He doesn't imply that too much homework was expected. Since Pete didn't study, we can assume he doesn't have a grasp on many different science topics. Pete was merely thinking of the many things that he needed to study.

7. **C**

    The author's purpose in this passage is to inform readers about chameleons. The author is not trying to entertain, instruct, or persuade.

8. **B**

    This is the best choice because the author introduces readers to chameleons and then continues by presenting details about chameleons' color-changing abilities, habitat, and threats.

9. D

The author compares the lizard walking on the branch to a tightrope walker at the circus to show the chameleon's agility. The comparison helps readers picture the lizard climbing a thin branch in the window of the pet shop.

10. D

When most people think of a magician, they picture a man or woman in a cape performing interesting tricks. Describing the lizard as a magician is a way of personifying the lizard.

11. C

Judging from the information surrounding this sentence, the author is trying to say that Shakespeare's work has been published all over the world.

12. B

The author discusses Shakespeare's life chronologically, beginning with his birth and ending with his death.

13. B

When the author explains that Shakespeare sharpened his skills, she means that he practiced until he got better.

14. A

Phrases such as "it is believed" and "it is thought," which begin each paragraph of the essay, show that the details of Shakespeare's life remain largely unknown and that most of what is known is speculation.

Chapter 3

Main Idea and Theme

Georgia Performance Standards

ELAALRL1 The student demonstrates comprehension by identifying evidence (e.g., diction, imagery, point of view, figurative language, symbolism, plot events, and main ideas) in a variety of texts representative of different genres (e.g., poetry, prose [short story, novel, essay, editorial, biography], and drama) and using this evidence as the basis for interpretation.

ELAALRL1.fiction. The student identifies, analyzes, and applies knowledge of the structures and elements of American fiction and provides evidence from the text to support understanding; the student

    c. relates identified elements in fiction to theme or underlying meaning.

ELAALRL2 The student identifies, analyzes, and applies knowledge of theme in a work of American literature and provides evidence from the work to support understanding. The student

    a. applies knowledge of the concept that the theme or meaning of a selection represents a universal view or comment on life or society and provides support from the text for the identified theme;

    b. evaluates the way an author's choice of words advances the theme or purpose of the work;

    c. applies knowledge of the concept that a text can contain more than one theme;

    d. analyzes and compares texts that express universal themes characteristic of American literature across time and genre (e.g., American individualism, the American dream, cultural diversity, and tolerance) and provides support from the texts for the identified themes.

Main Idea

The **main idea** of a passage is what it is mostly about. You'll be asked to identify the main idea of passages on the Georgia High School Graduation Test (GHSGT). Main idea questions on the GHSGT will most often follow nonfiction passages.

Some questions will ask you to choose a statement from the passage that best reflects the main idea of the passage. You may also be asked to choose a sentence not found in the passage that best describes the main idea of the passage. Usually, you won't be able to put your finger on the answers to these questions. You'll have to read the passage carefully and determine what it is mostly about or determine its most important points. Some answer choices may consist of details from the passage that do not represent the main idea of the passage. Others may represent incorrect interpretations of the main idea of a passage. It is helpful to note that the main idea of a passage is often given in the introduction. Sometimes the title will also offer a clue.

Theme

Theme is very similar to main idea. The **theme** of a passage is the overall idea in a literary work, or the message that is conveyed by the work. Some passages may contain more than one theme. GHSGT theme questions will follow fictional passages and poems.

Like GHSGT main idea questions, GHSGT questions on theme may ask you to choose a statement from the passage that best reflects the theme of the passage. Theme questions may also ask you to choose a sentence not in the passage that best describes the theme of the passage. If the theme is not stated in the passage, such as in fictional passages or poems, ask yourself what the story or poem is mostly about. Look for symbols that appear continually throughout the work. Sometimes the title can help you guess the theme as well. Make sure you choose the answer option that describes the overall idea of the passage. Stay away from options that simply describe a detail of the passage.

A passage will also contain supporting details, which are details that back up or confirm the main idea or theme. For most questions on supporting details, you will usually be able to look back at the passage to find the correct answer. On the GHSGT, you might be asked to choose a detail that best supports the main idea of the passage.

Questions for these standards will be multiple-choice (MC). Passages may be either fiction or nonfiction.

Passage 1

Read the following passage. Then answer the questions that follow. Use the Tip underneath each question to help you choose the correct answer. When you finish, read the answer explanations at the end of this chapter.

The Yellow Wallpaper
by Charlotte Perkins Gilman

We have been here two weeks, and I haven't felt like writing before, since that first day. I am sitting by the window now, up in this atrocious nursery, and there is nothing to hinder my writing as much as I please, save lack of strength.

John is away all day, and even some nights when his cases are serious. I am glad my case is not serious! But these nervous troubles are dreadfully depressing. John does not know how much I really suffer. He knows there is no REASON to suffer, and that satisfies him.

Of course it is only nervousness. It does weigh on me so not to do my duty in any way! I meant to be such a help to John, such a real rest and comfort, and here I am a comparative burden already!

Nobody would believe what an effort it is to do what little I am able,—to dress and entertain, and other things. It is fortunate Mary is so good with the baby. Such a dear baby! And yet I CANNOT be with him, it makes me so nervous.

I suppose John never was nervous in his life. He laughs at me so about this wall-paper! At first he meant to repaper the room, but afterwards he said that I was letting it get the better of me, and that nothing was worse for a nervous patient than to give way to such fancies.

He said that after the wall-paper was changed it would be the heavy bedstead, and then the barred windows, and then that gate at the head of the stairs, and so on. "You know the place is doing you good," he said, "and really, dear, I don't care to renovate the house just for a three months' rental."

"Then do let us go downstairs," I said, "there are such pretty rooms there." Then he took me in his arms and called me a blessed little goose, and said he would go down to the cellar, if I wished, and have it whitewashed into the bargain.

But he is right enough about the beds and windows and things. It is an airy and comfortable room as any one need wish, and, of course, I would not be so silly as to make him uncomfortable just for a whim. I'm really getting quite fond of the big room, all but that horrid paper. . . .

Out of one window I can see the garden, those mysterious deep-shaded arbors, the riotous old-fashioned flowers, and bushes and gnarly trees. Out of another I get a lovely view of the bay and a little private wharf belonging to the estate. There is a beautiful shaded lane that runs down there from the house. I always fancy I see people walking in these numerous paths and arbors, but John has cautioned me not to give way to fancy in the least. He says that with my imaginative power and habit of story-making, a nervous weakness like mine is sure to lead to all manner of excited fancies, and that I ought to use my will and good sense to check the tendency. So I try.

I think sometimes that if I were only well enough to write a little it would relieve the press of ideas and rest me. But I find I get pretty tired when I try. It is so discouraging not to have any advice and companionship about my work. When I get really well, John says we will ask Cousin Henry and Julia down for a long visit; but he says he would as soon put fireworks in my pillow-case as to let me have those stimulating people about now. I wish I could get well faster. But I must not think about that. This paper looks to me as if it KNEW what a vicious influence it had!

There is a recurrent spot where the pattern lolls like a broken neck and two bulbous eyes stare at you upside down. I get positively angry with the impertinence of it and the ever-lastingness. Up and down and sideways they crawl, and those absurd, unblinking eyes are everywhere. There is one place where two breadths didn't match, and the eyes go all up and down the line, one a little higher than the other. I never saw so much expression in an inanimate thing before, and we all know how much expression they have! I used to lie awake as a child and get more entertainment and terror out of blank walls and plain furniture than most children could find in a toy store. . . .

The wall-paper, as I said before, is torn off in spots, and it sticketh closer than a brother—they must have had perseverance as well as hatred. Then the floor is scratched and gouged and splintered, the plaster itself is dug out here and there, and this great heavy bed which is all we found in the room, looks as if it had been through the wars. But I don't mind it a bit—only the paper.

⃝? Questions

1. The passage illustrates which theme from American literature?

   A. Women can only be educated in captivity.

   B. Confinement is the worst cure for feminine mental illness.

   C. Women are foolish and must be imprisoned by men.

   D. Suppression of feminine expression is immoral.

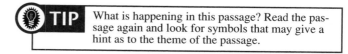

TIP What is happening in this passage? Read the passage again and look for symbols that may give a hint as to the theme of the passage.

2. Which statement from the passage **best** reflects the theme?

   A. "Of course it is only nervousness."

   B. "He laughs at me so about this wall-paper!"

   C. "I get positively angry with the impertinence of it and the everlastingness."

   D. "There is a beautiful shaded lane that runs down there from the house."

 TIP Which quote from the story illustrates the theme of the story? Consider the symbols you have noticed in the story, and then choose the quote that best reflects the meanings of those symbols.

3. Which idea **best** symbolizes the theme of the passage?

   A. The wallpaper is assisting with the narrator's repression.

   B. The narrator would be cured if the wallpaper was changed.

   C. The husband does not want to spend money on new wallpaper.

   D. The wallpaper is bringing the couple closer together.

 TIP Think about the wallpaper's role in the story. What does it represent? What is the author saying when she describes the wallpaper? Reread the passage and consider the function of the wallpaper in the story. How might it symbolize the theme?

Passage 2

Read the following passage. Then answer the questions that follow. Use the Tip underneath each question to help you choose the correct answer. When you finish, read the answer explanations at the end of this chapter.

Fuel of the Future
by Shelby Greene

Just because you don't see a biodiesel gas station on every street corner doesn't mean you shouldn't start making this fuel a part of your life. The cost of gas is on the rise. Many politicians are considering passing laws to freeze our use of fossil fuels because there simply aren't enough to go around. Biodiesel is becoming a viable option for powering our vehicles.

The government is creating all sorts of incentives to convince people to switch to biodiesel. One of these incentives is big tax breaks. Last year, U.S. production of biodiesel tripled. Politicians are getting behind biodiesel fuel partly manufactured from plants, because it solves two of our nation's biggest problems:

1. Americans can begin to break their addiction to fossil fuels.

2. Farmers are struggling. They will get a huge boost from the sudden surge in demand for their products.

The global warming debate has been heating up lately since scientists have discovered more evidence of global warming. More use of biofuel translates into fewer greenhouse gases in the air.

Even if there are no biodiesel distributors near you, biodiesel works in any diesel engine. One small but significant step you can take is to buy a diesel car instead of a car that runs on traditional unleaded gasoline. When the green revolution goes into full swing, you'll be ready. In field tests, cars powered by biodiesel have been shown to perform comparably to vehicles that run on traditional fuels. Contrary to what many people believe, biodiesel is distributed all over the United States, and the amount of stations where it is available is growing.

⑦ Questions

4. Which statement from the passage **best** reflects the main idea?

   A. "When the green revolution goes into full swing, you'll be ready."

   B. "Last year, U.S. production of biodiesel tripled."

   C. "One of these incentives is big tax breaks."

   D. "Biodiesel is becoming a viable option for powering our vehicles."

 The main idea of a passage is what it is mostly about. Which of these sentences from the passage describes what the passage is mostly about? Remember what you have learned about how a main idea is presented in a nonfiction passage.

5. Which **best** describes the main idea of the passage?

   A. We are depleting our fossil fuels by using unleaded gasoline.

   B. Biodiesel cannot be used in vehicles that use unleaded gasoline.

   C. Biodiesel is an environmentally friendly fuel alternative.

   D. We have many gas stations in this country that sell biofuel.

 Again, this question asks you to describe what this passage is mostly about. This question presents ideas that are discussed in the passage, rather than sentences that appear in the passage. Read each choice to determine which one represents the main idea and which ones are simply details from the passage.

6. Which detail **best** supports the main idea of the passage?

   A. Biodiesel emits fewer greenhouse gases than unleaded gasoline.

   B. Politicians want to stop people from using fossil fuels.

   C. The government gives tax breaks to those who switch to biodiesel fuel.

   D. Biodiesel fuel works in all vehicles with diesel engines.

 Once you have decided on the main idea of the passage, you must look for details that support the main idea to answer this question. What do you think the passage is mostly about? Which detail supports the main idea?

Passage 3

Read the following passage. Then answer the questions that follow. Use the Tip underneath each question to help you choose the correct answer. When you finish, read the answer explanations at the end of this chapter.

Logan's Lesson

Logan slammed the passenger door of his father's pickup truck and gazed warily at the main entrance of the Oceanside Nursing Home. He groaned inwardly and trudged toward the door, each step feeling heavier than the previous one.

Inside, Logan was greeted by a receptionist with a smile as sweet and syrupy as a Georgia peach and more perkiness in her greeting than Logan had been able to muster in his entire life. Her name tag said Suzanne. "You must be Logan," she chirped. "I can't *wait* for you to meet our residents."

Suzanne motioned for Logan to follow her, and he struggled to maintain the Olympic pace she set as she sped down a long corridor toward a set of double doors. A sign near the doors indicated that he was standing outside the Recreation Room. Peering through the window, Logan spied about a dozen silver-haired men and women in the room. Two men played a game of checkers in the corner, while another maneuvered a small scooter toward a rack of magazines. A few women sat in a circle of rocking chairs around a television watching a news program. One of them held yarn and knitting needles in her lap. On the far side of the room, one elderly man with white hair sat at a table by himself carving something from a small scrap of wood.

"That's Hector. I think you two will get along quite nicely," said Suzanne, pointing to the man at the far table.

Suzanne's pager began to beep, and after glancing at the numbers, she sprinted down the corridor. "I'm afraid you're on your own, Logan. I've got to get back to the reception area," she explained as she disappeared around the corner.

Logan sighed, shifted his backpack to his left shoulder, and shuffled toward Hector's table. As Logan extended his hand to introduce himself, Hector spoke. "Troublemaker, eh?"

Logan stepped back and withdrew his hand, the puzzled look on his face prompting Hector to continue.

"They always send me the troublemakers," he said, turning back to his wooden sculpture. "That, and your black eye gave you away."

Logan raised his hand to touch the painful bruise near his right eye. Hector's insights were correct. Logan's punishment for getting into a fight at school was to spend at least one hour every day at the nursing home until the end of the semester. Mr. Weatherby, the principal at Logan's high school, thought that spending time with some of the elderly residents at Oceanside would help him learn to care about others' thoughts and feelings.

Logan settled into the chair across from Hector. He watched silently as sawdust and shavings fell from the scrap of wood in Hector's wrinkled hands until finally, Hector set down his carving knife and placed the finished sculpture on the table. Logan carefully examined the petite form, amazed by the intricate details etched into the wood. It was a boxer wearing a helmet and boxing gloves, his feet slightly separated and his arms in a position indicating that he was ready to fight.

Logan glanced at Hector. "A fighter for a fighter," said the old man. With that, he lifted himself from his chair and moved toward the door.

"Wait," said Logan. "Aren't we supposed to talk or something?"

Hector turned around and winked, then disappeared through the double doors. Glancing at his watch, Logan realized that an hour had already passed and that his father would be waiting for him. He scooped the wooden figurine off the table, wrapped it in a tissue, and placed it in the zippered pouch of his backpack.

Logan remained quiet on the way home, reflecting on the unusual events of the afternoon. *Hector called me a troublemaker and a fighter*, he thought. It was a fitting description, but Logan had never intended to be either. It just seemed that sometimes, when someone or something made him angry or upset, he felt the need to release his anger, and the easiest way to do that was to punch, kick, or break something.

That night, Logan rummaged through his backpack until he found the boxer statue. Placing it on his desk, he stared at it for a long time. When he finally crawled into bed, he knew what he could discuss with Hector.

The next day, Logan looked for Hector in the Recreation Room, but he was nowhere to be found. Returning to the reception area, Logan ask Suzanne for directions to Hector's living quarters, but she informed him that Hector was on the balcony outside the craft room on the second floor. At the top of the steps, Logan made a left as Suzanne had instructed and walked the length of a blue hallway. He opened a door on the left and entered a room lined with shelves and overflowing with cans of paint, bottles of glue, stacks of paper, and a mishmash of other art supplies. Through the sliding door, Logan could see Hector standing at an easel, and beyond him, a magnificent view of the Atlantic Ocean.

"You paint, too," said Logan as he stepped outside.

Hector turned toward Logan, revealing a painting so similar to the ocean view Logan had just admired that the boy wondered if he was looking through an empty frame.

"What else do you do?" Logan asked.

Hector thought for a moment, and then explained that his numerous creative activities corresponded to how he felt at a particular point in time. When feeling happy or peaceful, he painted, and when feeling lonely or sad, he wrote poetry. When nervous, such as when he's about to meet someone new, he liked to whittle away at a piece of wood. Logan smiled, thinking of the wooden boxer. He was amazed by Hector's artistic abilities—poetry, paintings, drawings, sculptures, and carvings—each chosen to convey a certain mood, thought, or feeling.

"What do you do when you're angry?" asked Logan.

This time it was Hector who smiled. "I build things. Whether it's a chair, a table, or a simple puzzle, building things helps me release my anger *con*structively, rather than *de*structively," he explained.

Hector went inside to rinse his paintbrushes, and Logan contemplated what the old man had told him. A few minutes later, Logan joined Hector at the sink. "How do you release your emotions if you have no artistic abilities?" he asked. Like the day before, Hector winked and left Logan standing alone, filled with questions.

When Logan arrived at home, his mother yelled at him for forgetting to take the trash out. Later, his father grounded him because of Logan's poor showing on his history exam. Retiring to his room for the night, Logan then noticed that his sister's hamster had chewed a hole through one of his new sneakers. Logan could feel his anger building, but just as he was about to explode, he caught a glimpse of the wooden figurine on his desk.

Taking a deep breath, Logan thought of Hector. *Do something constructive, not destructive*, he said to himself. Looking around his room, Logan spied his guitar in the corner. He hadn't touched it in years, but something inside told him to pick it up and play. Sitting on the corner of his bed, he rested the guitar on his lap and began plucking the strings. Instantly, the storm that had been building inside him dissipated, and his shoulders relaxed.

Logan played cards with Hector in the Recreation Room the next day, and they exchanged stories about their families and friends. At the end of the hour, Logan hoisted his backpack and guitar case onto his shoulders, said goodbye, and started to walk away. When he reached the door, he turned around and winked at Hector.

"Thanks," he said.

? Questions

7. This passage illustrates which theme from American literature?

    A. embracing loss

    B. harnessing rage

    C. accepting regret

    D. admitting failure

 TIP What happens in this story? Consider what this story is mostly about, and then choose the theme that best applies to this story.

8. Which statement from the passage **best** reflects the theme?

   A. "Logan raised his hand to touch the painful bruise near his right eye."

   B. "*Hector called me a troublemaker and a fighter*, he thought."

   C. "*Do something constructive, not destructive*, he said to himself."

   D. " 'A fighter for a fighter,' said the old man."

 TIP Now that you've chosen the theme of the story, read it again, looking for evidence that supports the theme. Then choose the statement that best reflects the theme of the story.

9. Which idea **best** symbolizes the theme of the passage?

   A. Hector makes the wooden boxer to inspire Logan to start whittling wood.

   B. The wooden boxer helps Logan to stop and think before getting angry.

   C. Logan wants to be a proud fighter just like Hector's wooden boxer.

   D. The wooden boxer serves as proof that bad things happen to fighters.

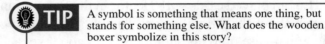 **TIP** A symbol is something that means one thing, but stands for something else. What does the wooden boxer symbolize in this story?

10. Which detail **best** supports the theme of the passage?

   A. Logan feels relaxed when he begins to play his guitar.

   B. Hector always winks at Logan when he leaves a room.

   C. Logan's father forces him to go to the nursing home.

   D. Hector's painting looks just like the Atlantic Ocean.

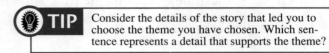 **TIP** Consider the details of the story that led you to choose the theme you have chosen. Which sentence represents a detail that supports the theme?

Passage 4

Read the following passage. Then answer the questions that follow. Use the Tip underneath each question to help you choose the correct answer. When you finish, read the answer explanations at the end of this chapter.

Tarantula Tamer

by Jacqueline Ray

If you ask Sidney Reich about her work, she will say her job is the greatest in the world—although most people would disagree. Sidney is a scientist specializing in the study and protection of the tarantula, a hairy creature that makes most people cringe.

Reich says her fascination with insects, particularly arachnids (insects with an exoskeleton), began when she was just a little girl. "I spent my early childhood in a rural town in Pennsylvania, where there weren't many children to play with. To occupy my time, I roamed the woods near my home, carefully studying every daddy longleg spider and tick I could find. I quickly observed that different types of spiders spun different types of webs, and I could seek out a spider simply by spotting its web. When I was about twelve, my family moved to California and I attended a much larger school. There I met many other kids who were interested in learning all about arachnids." Reich said she first saw a tarantula when hiking with a friend. "I could not believe my eyes! It was monstrous—a good three or four inches long—and the most incredible arthropod I had ever seen." Reich explained that the tarantula did not reciprocate her interest and quickly scooted back into its burrow, but this didn't matter; she was already hooked and wanted to learn as much about tarantulas as possible.

Today, Reich studies tarantulas in the rainforests throughout the world. Since tarantulas are nocturnal, Reich observes them at night when they are active. When asked if her work is dangerous, Reich confesses that she has had a few close calls, but not with tarantulas. She has suffered several snakebites and even a scorpion bite. But Reich considers her suffering worthwhile if her research helps save tarantulas, some species of which are in danger of extinction. She explains that when most people see a tarantula, they are so frightened that they step on it and kill it on the spot. "People don't realize that there is no record of a human ever dying from a tarantula bite and that most tarantulas hide from people rather than attack them." Reich blames horror movies for the tarantula's aggressive and deadly reputation. The destruction of the rainforests is another factor affecting the tarantula population. "The more people learn about tarantulas, the better off the spiders will be," Reich concludes. "People will begin to appreciate tarantulas as an important part of nature and will not want to harm them."

⁇ Questions

11. Which statement from the passage **best** reflects the main idea?

    A. "She has suffered several snakebites and even a scorpion bite."

    B. "The destruction of the rainforests is another factor affecting the tarantula population."

    C. "Today, Reich studies tarantulas in the rainforests throughout the world."

    D. "The more people learn about tarantulas, the better off the spiders will be."

 Consider what you have learned about finding the main idea in a passage. What main point is made in this passage? Which quote represents an idea that is stated throughout the passage?

12. Which **best** describes the main idea of the passage?

    A. Tarantulas do not want to harm humans and should not be killed.

    B. Some scientists have made a living by taming ferocious tarantulas.

    C. Reich is an expert in identifying different types of spiderwebs.

    D. California is the best place to learn all about arachnids.

 The main idea of a passage is what it is mostly about. Which of these sentences from the passage describes what the passage is mostly about? Remember what you have learned about how a main idea is presented in a nonfiction passage.

13. Which detail **best** supports the main idea of the passage?

    A. Rainforest destruction hurts tarantula populations.

    B. Most tarantulas hide from people rather than attack them.

    C. Different types of spiders spin different types of webs.

    D. Snakebites and scorpion bites are worse than tarantula bites.

 Now that you've decided on the main idea of the passage, choose the detail that best supports that main idea. Remember, a supporting detail backs up or confirms the main idea of a passage.

14. Which theme could **best** be applied to this passage?

    A. Time is a great teacher.

    B. History repeats itself.

    C. Ignorance breeds fear.

    D. Truth is hard to find.

 Consider the main idea and supporting details in this passage. Which theme relates to the main idea and supporting details of the passage?

 **Answers**

1. C

   In Victorian times, women were thought to be foolish and unintelligent. They were not encouraged to have their own opinions or feelings about life. The story suggests that the narrator's husband imprisoned her in the hopes of curing her of her nervous ideas and behaviors, which he thinks are silly. He thinks that she is weak, and that he can make her stronger by shutting her away from things that might cause her to have thoughts that he does not consider to be rational. At times, the narrator agrees with his views because society at this time did as well.

2. B

   You can tell that the husband thinks that the narrator is foolish when he laughs at her about the wallpaper. He thinks her ideas about the wallpaper are silly and that she is weak for letting it get the better of her. He pushes her to be stronger by forcing her to deal with the old wallpaper so that she will realize that she has been foolish about it. He does not understand that the wallpaper is worsening her mental state because he is not able to see logic in this idea.

3. A

   Because her husband has refused to change the wallpaper, and she cannot change it herself, the wallpaper comes to represent her repression and helplessness to change her situation. It becomes her prison because it is one of the few things she has to look at while she is captive in the room, and it is all around her. She eventually expresses her hatred for her situation by hating the wallpaper instead.

4. D

   This passage explains why biodiesel is becoming an attractive option for fueling our cars. It also explains why it has become more popular, as well as the fact that its use is already more widespread than people realize. The other answer choices simply cite details from the passage, but these details don't represent the main idea of the passage.

5. C

   The author is trying to convince people to use biodiesel because it is better for the environment. Its use results in the production of fewer greenhouse gases and will reduce our dependence on fossil fuels.

6. A

   The main idea of the passage is that biodiesel fuels are better for the environment than unleaded gasoline. This is because biodisel fuels emit fewer greenhouse gases, which are harmful to the environment.

7. B

   In this story, Logan learns that it is possible to harness rage so that he does not turn violent, and to instead use that energy to perform a useful activity.

8. C

   Logan's lesson is that when he feels anger building inside of him, he should do something constructive like building something or playing his guitar instead of something destructive like fighting or destroying something.

9. B

   At the end of the story, when Logan feels himself about to explode in anger, he looks at the wooden boxer and thinks of the lesson that he learned from Hector. By putting his energy into another activity (playing the guitar), he is able to stop himself from getting angry.

10. A

   Logan learns that harnessing his rage is a valuable skill when he begins to play his guitar and finds that it relaxes him.

11. D

   At the beginning of the passage, the author states that tarantulas make most people cringe. In the middle of the article, the author writes that Reich had never been threatened by a tarantula, and at the end of the article, Reich states that if people understood tarantulas, they would not want to harm them. This quote reinforces the point that tarantulas are not especially harmful to humans and therefore should not be killed.

12. A

   You can tell from the title of the passage that the passage will focus on tame tarantulas. Throughout the passage, both the author and Reich make points about people's unnecessary fear of tarantulas. The article also points out that many tarantulas are killed by people who are afraid of them, and that if people knew more about tarantulas, they would not want to harm them.

13. B

   The main idea of the passage is that tarantulas do not want to harm humans and should not be killed. The idea that most tarantulas hide from people rather than attack them supports this idea.

14. C

   The theme "Ignorance breeds fear" represents the idea that people who do not know about tarantulas are afraid of them because they think that the spiders will attack them.

Chapter 4

Author's Purpose

Georgia Performance Standards

ELAALRL1   The student demonstrates comprehension by identifying evidence (e.g., diction, imagery, point of view, figurative language, symbolism, plot events, and main ideas) in a variety of texts representative of different genres (e.g., poetry, prose [short story, novel, essay, editorial, biography], and drama) and using this evidence as the basis for interpretation.

ELAALRL1.fiction.   The student identifies, analyzes, and applies knowledge of the structures and elements of American fiction and provides evidence from the text to support understanding; the student

  d. analyzes, evaluates, and applies knowledge of the ways authors use techniques and elements in fiction for rhetorical and aesthetic purposes.

ELAALRL1.nonfiction.   The student identifies, analyzes, and applies knowledge of the purpose, structure, and elements of nonfiction and/or informational materials and provides evidence from the text to support understanding; the student

  b. analyzes and evaluates the logic and use of evidence in an author's argument;

  c. analyzes, evaluates, and applies knowledge of the ways authors use language, style, syntax, and rhetorical strategies for specific purposes in nonfiction works.

ELAALRL2   The student identifies, analyzes, and applies knowledge of theme in a work of American literature and provides evidence from the work to support understanding; the student

  b. evaluates the way an author's choice of words advances the theme or purpose of the work.

ELAALRL4   **The student employs a variety of writing genres to demonstrate a comprehensive grasp of significant ideas in sophisticated literary works. The student composes essays, narratives, poems, or technical documents. The student**

a. demonstrates awareness of an author's use of stylistic devices and an appreciation of the effects created by the devices;

b. analyzes the use of imagery, language, and other particular aspects of a text that contribute to theme or underlying meaning.

Author's Purpose for Writing

Some questions on the Georgia High School Graduation Test (GHSGT) will ask you to determine the reason an author may have written a passage. Authors may write short stories, novels, and poems to entertain their readers. They may write articles and nonfiction books that inform or describe a topic to readers. Authors write political speeches and letters to editors to persuade their readers to think as they do about an issue.

Some author's purpose questions on the GHSGT will ask you to identify the purpose of the text—to inform, persuade, entertain, or describe. Other questions will ask you about an author's opinion or point of view. For example, you may have to determine how an author feels about his or her subject matter. You may also be asked why an author writes a certain way or uses certain wording. For example, you might be asked why an author poses a question at the beginning of an essay. Some questions will ask you to identify an assertion that would best be supported by the information in the passage. You need to determine an author's opinion of the topic at hand to do this.

Passage 1

Read the following selection. Then answer the questions that follow. Use the Tip underneath each question to help you choose the correct answer. When you finish, read the answer explanations at the end of this chapter.

Don't Sweat Global Warming

Recently, scientists have suggested that Earth is experiencing its warmest temperatures in over a thousand years. This is fascinating and important news, but it has many people concerned. Some of these people view "global warming" as a major problem and want emergency laws to be passed in order to help reduce it. However, I believe that these people's concerns are unnecessary. Passing new global warming laws would do more harm than good to our world.

For several decades, scientists and concerned citizens have been exploring a theory called the "greenhouse effect." This theory holds that the warming of the planet is caused by human activity. Factories, automobiles, and certain household appliances cause harmful gases to drift into the sky. Some of these pollutants are called "greenhouse gases." They are believed to gather in the atmosphere and trap heat. Acting like a giant greenhouse, these gases cause the earth to grow warmer.

Believing greenhouse gases to be a main cause of global warming, many companies and countries joined together to reduce the amount of greenhouse gases they can legally emit. However, since then, leaders all over the world have begun to question the wisdom of this decision. The laws they passed create a burden on companies worldwide, and are not having a clear effect on global warming anyway.

It's clear that the planet *is* getting warmer. Average temperatures rise each year, and instances of record-breaking heat are more and more common. Also, there have been many unusual occurrences in the weather that may be tied to this warming, such as floods, droughts, and storms.

What is *not* clear is that human beings are the cause of this warming. I feel that greenhouse gases and other air pollution, while being dangerous and harmful to our planet, are not the cause of global warming. In fact, global warming is probably caused by Earth itself. Throughout the history of the world, temperatures have changed, sometimes significantly. There were times of blistering heat, as well as freezing Ice Ages, long before humans even existed. There was even a "mini Ice Age" as recently as a few hundred years ago. The Earth's temperature simply changes for reasons that are far beyond people's control.

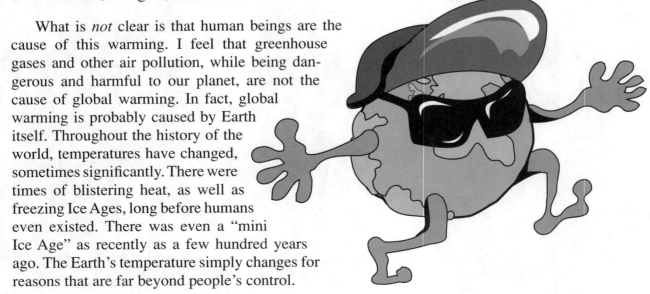

People who still believe that greenhouse gases cause global warming have been pushing for new laws to reduce these gases. These laws would be aimed at changing the fuels we use and regulating, or even shutting down, businesses that emit greenhouse gases.

If these laws were passed, it would be a disaster for our economy. These laws would force many important businesses to stop production while they removed greenhouse gases from their factories. This "cleanup" might take weeks or months, during which time the companies could lose millions of dollars. Meanwhile, consumers would be deprived of the companies' products.

Additionally, the effect of such laws on many foreign economies could be downright devastating. The United States has many computer-based technological businesses that wouldn't be altered by these laws. However, many other nations, especially developing ones, *rely* on factories. If their factories were shut down, these countries would lose an essential part of their economy and society. This would be tragic, especially since most greenhouse gases are produced by the United States and other, wealthier nations. Less fortunate countries would be made to suffer for the mistakes and misdeeds of Americans—is that fair?

Even if these laws were put into effect and the world economy survived them, there is no guarantee that the laws would yield any positive results. Let's say that alternative sources of fuel and energy that do not produce greenhouse gases are put into widespread use. Who can say if these fuels will be effective? Also, almost every kind of fuel will have some harmful by-product. Just because one type of energy doesn't leave behind greenhouse gases doesn't mean it's safe for the environment. For instance, nuclear power leaves behind poisonous nuclear wastes; even the so-called cleanest energies, solar and wind power, require the deforestation of large amounts of land. No kind of power is perfect, and the fuels that cause greenhouse gases are by no means the worst.

Despite these many reasonable objections to anti-greenhouse gas laws, many people continue to push for them. These people insist that greenhouse gases cause global warming, and that global warming will culminate in global disaster. This idea has no foundation at all. As mentioned earlier, the temperature on Earth rises and falls naturally. There are cold periods and warm periods that occur randomly and without any sort of human interference. Global warming is natural and will not destroy the planet or its inhabitants.

People are continually overestimating the possible dangers of global warming and the effects of greenhouse gases. They claim that the heating of the planet may cause diseases like malaria to spread, kill vegetation and the animals that rely on it, encourage wildfires, and melt the polar ice caps. The final point is considered the most dangerous. If the polar ice caps melted, more water would be added to the oceans, causing them to rise. This can cause massive, deadly floods and would have the potential to permanently cover entire countries with water. These claims sound compelling, but they aren't realistic.

The situation is nowhere near as bad as many people insist. As scientists learn more and more about the warming of our planet, they continually realize that the effects of the warming won't be so dangerous. Only minute changes will take place, even over the course of many hundreds of years. There will be no sudden catastrophes because of global warming.

The Earth is indeed warming, but it is a slow and entirely natural process. Global warming will not lead to disasters, and it is not caused by anything humans are doing or failing to do. People can pass thousands of laws to regulate factories, cars, and any other human-made objects, but this will have no effect on global warming. These laws will only make life harder for the people of Earth.

? Questions

1. What assertion is **best** supported by the evidence in the passage?

   A. Global warming is an unnatural result of pollution.

   B. Global warming may cause diseases in humans.

   C. Global warming is not as serious as people think.

   D. Global warming should be controlled by legislation.

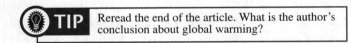

TIP Reread the end of the article. What is the author's conclusion about global warming?

2. The phrase "will culminate in global disaster" implies that

   A. global disaster can be easily prevented.

   B. global warming will lead to global disaster.

   C. global disaster has already occurred.

   D. global warming is the same as global disaster.

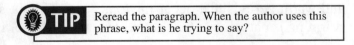

TIP Reread the paragraph. When the author uses this phrase, what is he trying to say?

3. Which technique does the author use to instruct readers in paragraphs 5 through 9?

   A. speaking directly to readers

   B. providing historical examples

   C. giving questions and answers

   D. writing in technical jargon

TIP Skim over these paragraphs in the passage. In what way does the author try to inform the reader?

Passage 2

Read the following selection. Then answer the questions that follow. Use the Tip underneath each question to help you choose the correct answer. When you finish, read the answer explanations at the end of this chapter.

The Hypnotist
by Ambrose Bierce

My first knowledge that I possessed unusual powers came to me in my fourteenth year, when at school. Happening one day to have forgotten to bring my noon-day luncheon, I gazed longingly at that of a small girl who was preparing to eat hers. Looking up, her eyes met mine and she seemed unable to withdraw them. After a moment of hesitancy she came forward in an absent kind of way and without a word surrendered her little basket with its tempting contents and walked away. Inexpressibly pleased, I relieved my hunger and destroyed the basket. After that I had not the trouble to bring a luncheon for myself: that little girl was my daily purveyor. . . . The girl was always persuaded that she had eaten all herself; and later in the day her tearful complaints of hunger surprised the teacher, entertained the pupils, earned for her the sobriquet of Greedy-Gut and filled me with a peace past understanding. . . .

For some years afterward I had little opportunity to practice hypnotism; such small essays as I made at it were commonly barren of other recognition than solitary confinement on a bread-and-water diet; sometimes, indeed, they elicited nothing better than the cat-o'-nine-tails. It was when I was about to leave the scene of these small disappointments that my one really important feat was performed.

I had been called into the warden's office and given a suit of civilian's clothing, a trifling sum of money and a great deal of advice, which I am bound to confess was of a much better quality than the clothing. As I was passing out of the gate into the light of freedom I suddenly turned and looking the warden gravely in the eye, soon had him in control.

"You are an ostrich," I said.

At the post-mortem examination the stomach was found to contain a great quantity of indigestible articles mostly of wood or metal. Stuck fast in the esophagus and constituting, according to the Coroner's jury, the immediate cause of death, one door-knob.

I was by nature a good and affectionate son, but as I took my way into the great world from which I had been so long secluded I could not help remembering that all my misfortunes had flowed like a stream from … my parents in the matter of school luncheons; and I knew of no reason to think they had reformed. . . .

It was while going afoot to South Asphyxia, the home of my childhood, that I found both my parents on their way to the Hill. They had hitched their team and were eating luncheon under an oak tree in the center of the field. The sight of the luncheon called up painful memories of my school days and roused the sleeping lion in my breast.

Approaching the guilty couple, who at once recognized me, I ventured to suggest that I share their hospitality.

"Of this cheer, my son," said the author of my being, with characteristic pomposity, which age had not withered, "there is sufficient for but two. I am not, I hope, insensible to the hunger-light in your eyes, but—"

My father has never completed that sentence; what he mistook for hunger-light was simply the earnest gaze of the hypnotist. In a few seconds he was at my service. A few more sufficed for the lady, and the dictates of a just resentment could be carried into effect. "My former father," I said, "I presume that it is known to you that you and this lady are no longer what you were?"

"I have observed a certain subtle change," was the rather dubious reply of the old gentleman; "it is perhaps attributable to age."

"It is more than that," I explained; "it goes to character—to species. You and the lady here are, in truth, two broncos—wild stallions both, and unfriendly."

"Why, John," exclaimed my dear mother, "you don't mean to say that I am—"

"Madam," I replied, solemnly, fixing my eyes again upon hers, "you are."

Scarcely had the words fallen from my lips when she dropped upon her hands and knees, and backing up to the old man squealed like a demon and delivered a vicious kick upon his shin! An instant later he was himself down on all-fours, headed away from her and flinging his feet. . . . With equal earnestness but inferior agility, because of her hampering body-gear, she plied her own. Their flying legs crossed and mingled in the most bewildering way. . . . On recovering themselves they would resume the combat, uttering their frenzy in the nameless sounds of the furious brutes which they believed themselves to be—the whole region rang with their clamor! . . . Wild, inarticulate screams of rage attested the delivery of the blows; groans, grunts and gasps their receipt. Nothing more truly military was ever seen at Gettysburg or Waterloo: the valor of my dear parents in the hour of danger can never cease to be to me a source of pride and gratification. . . .

Arrested for provoking a breach of the peace, I was, and have ever since been, tried in the Court of Technicalities and Continuances whence, after fifteen years of proceedings, my attorney is moving heaven and earth to get the case taken to the Court of Remandment for New Trials.

Such are a few of my principal experiments in the mysterious force or agency known as hypnotic suggestion. Whether or not it could be employed by a bad man for an unworthy purpose I am unable to say.

 Questions

4. The phrase "roused the sleeping lion in my breast" is a metaphor for

   A. how anger developed inside the narrator.

   B. how the narrator behaved like a lion.

   C. the narrator turning his parents into animals.

   D. the narrator's happiness at seeing his parents.

TIP Reread the paragraph. Then, think about lions and what they might symbolize. What is the author trying to get across with this metaphor?

5. At the end of the passage, the narrator's statement about the possible use of his powers is an example of what literary device?

   A. irony

   B. symbolism

   C. hyperbole

   D. personification

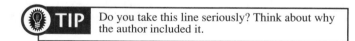

TIP Do you take this line seriously? Think about why the author included it.

6. Which assertion is **best** supported by the evidence in the passage?

   A. The narrator is embarrassed by his parents' special powers.

   B. The narrator thinks his parents did a decent job raising him.

   C. The narrator feels that his parents are incredibly intelligent.

   D. The narrator is mad at his parents for not being generous.

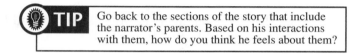

TIP Go back to the sections of the story that include the narrator's parents. Based on his interactions with them, how do you think he feels about them?

Passage 3

Read the following selection. Then answer the questions that follow. Use the Tip underneath each question to help you choose the correct answer. When you finish, read the answer explanations at the end of this chapter.

The Truth about Year-Round Education
by Rebecca Simonson

No More Teachers, No More Books . . .

Summer. For many students, summer means a vacation with their families, time to relax with their friends, or an opportunity to make some extra money at a summer job. But, believe it or not, summer still means school for some students. These kids aren't attending classes because of poor grades or to try to get ahead, but because their school district runs on the innovative year-round schedule.

The traditional ten-month school schedule that most students are accustomed to was formed during a time when many Americans lived on farms. During the summer, children were needed to help their families work the fields and prepare for the fall harvest. Even after farming declined, many schools stuck with the original schedule because many felt that it was too hot to keep students cooped up inside all day during a time when many schools lacked air-conditioning systems. However, in recent years there has been a movement to institute year-round education in school districts throughout the United States.

How Year-Round Education Really Works

Despite what many people think, many students who go to school year-round don't spend more days in class than children that attend traditional schools. Besides the extended school-year program, which considerably lengthens the time that children spend in school, most students in year-round programs spend the traditional 170 to 180 days in class, but their vacation time is broken up throughout the year.

Some schools use a single-track system. This means that all students and faculty are in session and take breaks all at the same time. This system has several subsystems that include a flexible all-year calendar that allows students and teachers to take short breaks when it is convenient for them. Modified schedules are also used in this system. Some schools will have forty-five days of instruction followed by a fifteen-day break, while others keep students and teachers in class for ninety days and then break for thirty days.

Multitrack systems are also used in year-round education, usually by schools that have overcrowding issues. Multitrack systems usually have three to five tracks and each student is assigned to a specific track. While students in certain tracks are in school, the students in one or two other tracks will be on vacation. This is generally used so that a school can house more students without having to build new schools or shipping students to other districts.

Benefits

Besides allowing school districts to accommodate an ever-growing number of students, year-round education is thought to have many more benefits. Some argue that cutting out the long summer break decreases the amount of information students lose while not receiving instruction. This allows teachers to focus more on new material rather than wasting time reviewing at the beginning of the year.

Others feel that more frequent breaks mean that both students and teachers will be absent less often because this schedule allows for time to rest and relax during the school year. Another appealing aspect to the unorthodox system is that the program not only helps to alleviate overcrowding, but may also save taxpayers money that would need to be spent creating new schools and hiring faculty. Supporters of the system also argue that year-round education is used throughout the world in many countries where students perform better academically than their U.S. counterparts.

Drawbacks

Of course, there are those that believe that a year-round school system isn't the answer to America's educational problems. Critics argue that doing away with summer vacation will greatly disrupt many families' social schedules. Parents of young children will have to find someone to watch their kids during these short breaks since they cannot attend camp or day care that is usually offered during the summer months. Also, many feel that extracurricular activities would suffer under the year-round education system. Sports and music events often require interaction between school districts. If one school is year-round and the other is not, scheduling a time for such activities could be very difficult.

The most important argument against the system is that there is no statistically significant evidence showing that year-round education improves students' academic abilities or increases standardized test scores. Supporters argue that this is not the case, but critics point to several studies that show only minor improvements in students participating in year-round education.

So Long, Summer?

According to the National Association for Year-Round Education, 3,181 American schools had adopted this alternative educational system by the 2002–2003 school year, including three school districts in Florida. Does this mean that students should live in fear of the day when their summers are no longer their own? Well, let's just say that they shouldn't throw in their beach towels just yet.

Parents, teachers, and students across the United States continue to debate the positive and negative aspects of the program. The topic remains a controversial one, and many school districts have opposed a switch. But, the truth is, American students continue to lag behind children in Europe and Asia academically. Perhaps a little less fun in the sun, and a little more time in the classroom, might be just what students need to help them get ahead.

⑦ Questions

7. The author writes that

    . . . this allows teachers to focus more on new material rather than wasting time reviewing at the beginning of the year.

    The **most likely** reason the author chose these words would be to

    A. imply that reviewing old material is useless.

    B. promote year-round schooling as beneficial.

    C. accuse teachers of wasting students' time.

    D. show that traditional schools have deteriorated.

    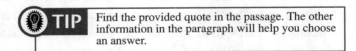 Find the provided quote in the passage. The other information in the paragraph will help you choose an answer.

8. The words *innovative*, *unorthodox*, *alternative*, and *controversial* all are used to describe the year-round schedule. Which word would a writer or speaker use to express support for the system?

    A. innovative

    B. unorthodox

    C. alternative

    D. controversial

     Think about each word's connotation, the traditional feelings that are associated with it. Which word would a person who supports year-round schooling use?

9. In the passage, the author includes drawbacks to year-round education in order to

    A. prove that year-round schooling is detrimental to extracurricular activities.

    B. provide balanced information about the question of year-round schooling.

    C. suggest it would be bad for all schools to switch to year-round schooling.

    D. connect year-round schooling to improved academic abilities in students.

 You have to analyze the information in the article to answer this question. Reread the article, and then review your choices. Which of these does the author do?

10. Which assertion is **best** supported by the evidence in this passage?

    A. Schools in warm areas should close for summer.

    B. A single-track system produces better students.

    C. A multitrack system prohibits teachers' breaks.

    D. Year-round schooling might work for some schools.

 Think about why the author wrote this article. How does she feel about her subject matter? How does she want her reader to feel about her topic?

Passage 4

Read the following selection. Then answer the questions that follow. Use the Tip underneath each question to help you choose the correct answer. When you finish, read the answer explanations at the end of this chapter.

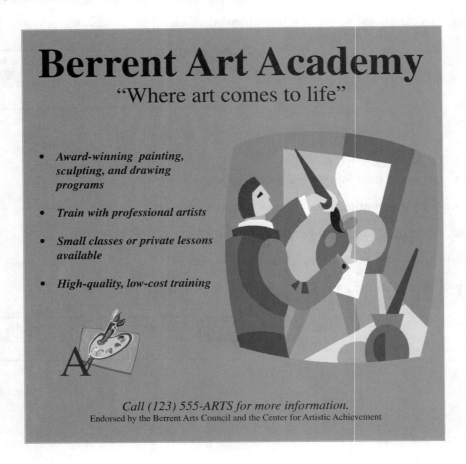

? Questions

11. To which audience is the advertisement directed?

    A. professional artists

    B. amateur artists

    C. art teachers

    D. art critics

 TIP   Read the advertisement closely.

12. The phrase "art comes to life" is a metaphor for

    A. improving artwork.

    B. art being important.

    C. creating artwork.

    D. art imitating life.

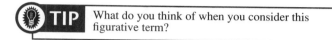
TIP What do you think of when you consider this figurative term?

13. What is **most likely** the reason the organizations have endorsed this academy?

    A. They want art educators to become certified before teaching classes.

    B. They believe that the programs will guarantee success as an artist.

    C. They assert that the academy provides an excellent art education.

    D. They award prizes to the academy for its various art programs.

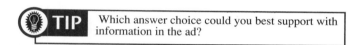
TIP Which answer choice could you best support with information in the ad?

14. The author created this advertisement in order to

    A. express an opinion about the value of art.

    B. tell a story about a talented artist.

    C. inform readers about different types of art.

    D. persuade readers to take art classes.

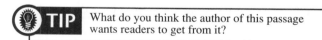
TIP What do you think the author of this passage wants readers to get from it?

✔ Answers

1. C

   The author clearly indicates that people are too concerned with global warming and that it's not as serious as people think.

2. B

   Culminate means *to conclude or end*. In this statement, the narrator is saying that global warming will lead to a global disaster.

3. B

   The author provides the reader with examples of the earth heating and cooling throughout history.

4. A

   The author uses this metaphor to describe how the anger was set in motion inside of him.

5. A

   The final statement by the narrator conveys how he has no remorse for his actions. Such an ironic statement sheds a humorous light on all of the narrator's prior actions.

6. D

   The author mentions in the middle of the story that he blames his parents' not giving him big enough lunches for the horrible things he does in his life. Later, when his parents won't share their picnic with him, he feels his anger at them anew.

7. B

   The author does not argue that traditional schools are particularly bad, but she does point out the benefits of year-round schooling.

8. A

   The word *alternative* doesn't have strong negative or positive connotations, but *unorthodox* and *controversial* could both be taken negatively. *Innovative* has positive connotations and would most likely be used in support of something.

9. B

   Judging from the final statement in the essay, the author seems to support year-round schooling. She most likely included the drawbacks to provide a fair and balanced argument.

10. D

The author doesn't indicate that all schools should adopt a year-round education system, but she thinks it is something they should consider.

11. B

The advertisement caters to amateur artists. It says that students will be taught by professional artists, so Answer Choices A, B, and D are not the best answer.

12. C

The phrase "art coming to life" means that something goes from merely an idea to a real, tangible thing.

13. C

Of the answer choices, only choice C states a conclusion that can be made from the information provided.

14. D

This ad is trying to convince readers that the best place to take art lessons is at Berrent Art Academy.

Chapter 5

Elements of Fiction

Georgia Performance Standards

ELAALRL1   The student demonstrates comprehension by identifying evidence (e.g., diction, imagery, point of view, figurative language, symbolism, plot events, and main ideas) in a variety of texts representative of different genres (e.g., poetry, prose [short story, novel, essay, editorial, biography], and drama) and using this evidence as the basis for interpretation.

ELAALRL1.fiction.   The student identifies, analyzes, and applies knowledge of the structures and elements of American fiction and provides evidence from the text to support understanding; the student

   a. locates and analyzes such elements in fiction as language and style, character development, point of view, irony, and structures (e.g., chronological, in medias res, flashback, frame narrative, epistolary novel) in works of American fiction from different time periods;

   b. identifies and analyzes patterns of imagery or symbolism;

   c. relates identified elements in fiction to theme or underlying meaning;

   d. Analyzes, evaluates, and applies knowledge of the ways authors use techniques and elements in fiction for rhetorical and aesthetic purposes.

   e. analyzes the influence of mythic, traditional, or classical literature on American literature;

   f. traces the history of the development of American fiction.

ELAALRL2. The student identifies, analyzes, and applies knowledge of theme in a work of American literature and provides evidence from the work to support understanding. The student

   a. applies knowledge of the concept that the theme or meaning of a selection represents a universal view or comment on life or society and provides support from the text for the identified theme;

   b. evaluates the way an author's choice of words advances the theme or purpose of the work;

c. applies knowledge of the concept that a text can contain more than one theme;

d. analyzes and compares texts that express universal themes characteristic of American literature across time and genre (e.g., American individualism, the American dream, cultural diversity, and tolerance) and provides support from the texts for the identified themes.

ELAALRL3. The student deepens understanding of literary works by relating them to their contemporary context or historical background, as well as to works from other time periods.

The student relates a literary work to primary source documents of its literary period or historical setting; the student

a. relates a literary work to the seminal ideas of the time in which it is set or the time of its composition:

  i. Native American literature

  ii. Colonial/Revolutionary/National literature

b. relates a literary work to the characteristics of the literary time period that it represents:

  i. Romanticism/transcendentalism

  ii. Realism

  iii. Naturalism

  iv. Modernism (including Harlem Renaissance)

  v. Postmodernism

The student compares and contrasts specific characteristics of different genres as they develop and change over time for different purposes (e.g., personal, meditative Colonial writing vs. public, political documents of the Revolutionary era, or replication of traditional European styles [Bradstreet, Taylor] vs. emerging distinctive American style [Dickinson, Whitman] in poetry).

The student analyzes a variety of works representative of different genres within specific time periods in order to identify types of discourse (e.g., satire, parody, allegory, pastoral) that cross the lines of genre classifications.

Questions on the Georgia High School Graduation Test (GHSGT) that address fiction will ask about short stories and excerpts from novels. They will be multiple-choice and will focus on three main areas: interpretation, context, and theme.

Interpretation

To answer the fiction questions on the GHSGT, you should be familiar with the elements of American fiction, such as diction, language, style, imagery, point of view, figurative language, irony, character development, symbolism, plot, mood, and main idea. Questions might ask you whether one of these elements is used in a passage. You might also be asked which event in a passage is an example of one of these elements. Questions on literary elements might ask you why an author used a certain technique or element of fiction in his or her writing.

You should also be familiar with the traditional structures of American fiction such as chronological, in medias res, flashback, foreshadowing, frame narrative, or epistolary novels. Questions on literary interpretation might ask you to explain the underlying meaning of a text.

Often these questions will ask about the influence that mythic, traditional, or classical literature has on American fiction. They might also ask about the history of American fiction and how American fiction has changed over time.

Context

Questions on the test may ask you to connect a text—such as a passage from Native American, Colonial and Revolutionary, or National literature—to its historical context. To answer these questions, examine the text for clues that it reveals about the culture of the time in which it was written. These questions might ask about ideas that were popular during the time in which the passage was written and how these ideas are evident in the passage.

Questions might also ask about the characteristics of literary time periods, for instance, romanticism, transcendentalism, realism, naturalism, modernism (including the Harlem Renaissance), and postmodernism. These questions might ask you to identify which period a passage belongs to and to use details from the passage as evidence. Questions might also present a characteristic of American fiction and ask which literary time period it belongs to.

Theme

Questions might ask you to identify the theme (the comment the passage makes about life) or themes in the passage and to use details from the text as evidence. Questions might ask how an author's choice of words reveals the theme of the passage. You also might be asked to compare the themes of multiple works, especially works that employ common themes in American fiction such as individualism, the American dream, cultural diversity, and tolerance.

Passage 1

Read the following passage. Then answer the questions that follow. Use the Tip underneath each question to help you choose the correct answer. When you finish, read the answer explanations at the end of this chapter.

Ripe Figs

by Kate Chopin

Maman-Nainaine said that when the figs were ripe Babette might go to visit her cousins down on Bayou-Boeuf, where the sugar cane grows. Not that the ripening of figs had the least thing to do with it, but that is the way Maman-Nainaine was.

It seemed to Babette a very long time to wait; for the leaves upon the trees were tender yet, and the figs were like little hard, green marbles.

But warm rains came along and plenty of strong sunshine; and though Maman-Nainaine was as patient as the statue of la Madone, and Babette as restless as a humming-bird, the first thing they both knew it was hot summer-time. Every day Babette danced out to where the fig-trees were in a long line against the fence. She walked slowly beneath them, carefully peering between the gnarled, spreading branches. But each time she came disconsolate away again. What she saw there finally was something that made her sing and dance the whole day long.

When Maman-Nainaine sat down in her stately way to breakfast the following morning, her muslin cap standing like an aureole about her white, placid face, Babette approached. She bore a dainty porcelain platter, which she set down before her godmother. It contained a dozen purple figs, fringed around with their rich, green leaves.

"Ah," said Maman-Nainaine, arching her eyebrows, "how early the figs have ripened this year!"

"Oh," said Babette, "I think they have ripened very late."

"Babette," continued Maman-Nainaine, as she peeled the very plumpest figs with her pointed silver fruit-knife, "you will carry my love to them all down on Bayou-Boeuf. And tell your tante Frosine I shall look for her at Toussaint—when the chrysanthemums are in bloom."

(?) Questions

1. The point of view used in the passage reveals

   A. Maman-Nainaine's anger at the cousins.

   B. Babette's excitement with leaving soon.

   C. Maman-Nainaine's misery with Babette.

   D. Babette's enjoyment of watching the figs.

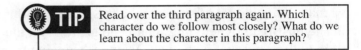

TIP   Read over the third paragraph again. Which character do we follow most closely? What do we learn about the character in this paragraph?

2. Which sentence **best** describes the theme of this passage?

   A. We appreciate things more if we wait for them.

   B. Figs take an awfully long time to become ripe.

   C. Looking forward to something is entertaining.

   D. It is really important to learn to have patience.

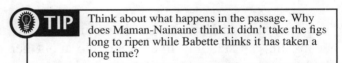

TIP   Think about what happens in the passage. Why does Maman-Nainaine think it didn't take the figs long to ripen while Babette thinks it has taken a long time?

3. What is the **most likely** reason Maman-Nainaine tells Babette to wait until the figs ripen?

   A. She wants Babette to ignore her own family.

   B. She doesn't like when Babette does fun things.

   C. She doesn't want Babette to travel until summer.

   D. She wants Babette to serve the ripened figs to her.

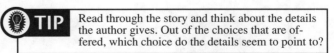

TIP   Read through the story and think about the details the author gives. Out of the choices that are offered, which choice do the details seem to point to?

Passage 2

Read the following passage. Then answer the questions that follow. Use the Tip underneath each question to help you choose the correct answer. When you finish, read the answer explanations at the end of this chapter.

The Thinking Spot

It was a Saturday afternoon and I was supposed to be writing a journal entry for Monday's English class about my fondest childhood memory. Unfortunately, the rhythmic blinking of the cursor was the only movement on my otherwise blank computer screen. Frustrated, I let my eyes wander to the window. The mammoth oak tree in my backyard dominated most of the view. Fresh leaves the vivid green of spring fluttered in the breeze and the old swing that hung from the tree's largest branch gently swayed back and forth. "My thinking spot," I said aloud. Leaving all thoughts of homework assignments behind, I went outside.

I circled the old swing several times, tugging the ropes to make sure they weren't rotted and rubbing my hand across the wooden seat to check for splinters. Rendering it safe for use, I hoisted myself onto the seat and pumped my legs back and forth. Though it had probably been six or seven years since my last outing on the swing, the pendulum-like motion felt familiar and comfortable. I remembered why this had once been my favorite location to sit and contemplate the world. As the swing traveled back and forth, my mind opened and thoughts deluged my brain.

Suddenly, I was five years old again, begging my grandpa to push me on the swing. "C'mon, Gramp," I would plead, adding the one phrase I knew he couldn't resist: "Pretty please with a cherry on top." Whether it was the missing front tooth in my awkward smile or the unraveling braids I wore in my brown hair, Gramp would grin and crumble and I would have my way. Within minutes, we would traipse hand-in-hand across the dew-covered lawn toward the swing.

"Hold on tight," he would say, as he gave the swing a hefty push to get it started. I would smile and giggle as the swing flew higher and higher into the air. Soon, I could see over the Millers' fence, right into their pool, and catch a glimpse of the football stuck in the Carmichaels' gutter. I could see the patch of shingles on the roof of my house where Dad had patched a leak during a rainstorm. Wispy strands of hair would fly away from my face, and then tickle my cheeks and forehead as the swing moved forward and backward.

As darkness fell, Gramp would slow the swing to a stop and lift me onto his shoulders. We would return to the house, following the dim glow cast from the kitchen window. Once inside, Gramp would settle into an armchair, I would climb into his lap, and he would read me a book of children's poems by Robert Louis Stevenson. When he reached my favorite rhyme, I would recite it right along with him: "Oh how I love to go up in a swing . . ."

When Gramp wasn't around, sometimes I could convince my older brother, George, to push me on the swing. George's technique was much different than Gramp's. Instead of starting out slow and allowing the swing to steadily fly higher and higher, George would pull the swing as far back and as high as he could—sometimes I felt like I might slip right out of the seat!—and then he would run, full speed, right underneath the swing. "Underdog!" he would yell as he released the ropes, and I would shriek with a combination of excited delight and fear that I would swing upside-down, right over the tree branch.

By the time I was nine years old, Gramp had moved into a nursing home and George had gotten his driver's license and wasn't home much. It was up to me to get my swing moving faster and higher, and to create my own thrilling adventures. In my mind, my swing had been my spaceship, rocketing around the universe at record speeds, and my Pegasus, the flying horse of Greek mythology. It had been my trapeze, my time machine, and the dragon I had tamed as the world's fiercest female knight. But most of all, my swing had been my "thinking spot," the one place where I knew I could completely lose myself in thought. Riding my swing, I must have composed thousands of songs and poems, and hundreds of scenarios for my friends and me to act out.

That Saturday on the swing was no different. As I scuffed my feet through the worn patch of grass beneath the swing and gradually came to a stop, I felt as though I had accomplished the impossible. Returning to my computer, my fingers danced across the keyboard and I watched as the screen filled with the fondest memory from my childhood: my thinking spot.

Questions

4. Which **best** describes the way in which the passage is structured?

    A. a conflict followed by a resolution

    B. details describing a character

    C. main idea with anecdotes

    D. a sequence of events

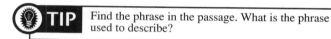

> **TIP** If you can't decide which answer choice is correct, write a brief summary of the passage. Then compare the summary to each answer choice.

5. The phrase "pendulum-like motion" is a simile for

    A. soothing speech.

    B. repetitive movement.

    C. comforting memories.

    D. passing of time.

> **TIP** Find the phrase in the passage. What is the phrase used to describe?

6. The narrator wrote,

    It was up to me to get my swing moving faster and higher, and to create my own thrilling adventures.

    The **most likely** reason the narrator chose these words would be to

    A. try to show that she became very lonely.

    B. imply that she swung better by herself.

    C. try to show that she missed her brother.

    D. imply that she grew more independent.

> **TIP** Tip: Remember that the narrator is grown now, so she wouldn't need someone to push her on the swing.

Passage 3

Read the following passage. Then answer the questions that follow. Use the Tip underneath each question to help you choose the correct answer. When you finish, read the answer explanations at the end of this chapter.

Excerpt from "The False Gems"
by Guy de Maupassant

Monsieur Lantin had met the young girl at a reception at the house of the second head of his department, and had fallen head over heels in love with her. . . . She and her mother came to live in Paris, where the latter, who made the acquaintance of some of the families in her neighborhood, hoped to find a husband for her daughter.

They had very moderate means, and were honorable, gentle, and quiet.

The young girl was a perfect type of the virtuous woman in whose hands every sensible young man dreams of one day intrusting his happiness. Her simple beauty had the charm of angelic modesty, and the imperceptible smile which constantly hovered about the lips seemed to be the reflection of a pure and lovely soul.

Monsieur Lantin . . . enjoyed a snug little salary of three thousand five hundred francs, and he proposed to this model young girl, and was accepted.

She governed his household with such clever economy that they seemed to live in luxury. She lavished the most delicate attentions on her husband, coaxed and fondled him; and so great was her charm that six years after their marriage, Monsieur Lantin discovered that he loved his wife even more than during the first days of their honeymoon.

He found fault with only two of her tastes: Her love for the theatre, and her taste for imitation jewelry. Her friends (the wives of some petty officials) frequently procured for her a box at the theatre, often for the first representations of the new plays; and her husband was obliged to accompany her, whether he wished it or not, to these entertainments which bored him excessively after his day's work at the office.

After a time, Monsieur Lantin begged his wife to request some lady of her acquaintance to accompany her, and to bring her home after the theatre.

Now, with her love for the theatre, came also the desire for ornaments. Her costumes remained as before, simple, in good taste, and always modest; but she soon began to adorn her ears with huge rhinestones, which glittered and sparkled like real diamonds.

Her husband frequently remonstrated with her, saying:

"My dear, as you cannot afford to buy real jewelry, you ought to appear adorned with your beauty and modesty alone, which are the rarest ornaments of your sex."

But she would smile sweetly, and say:

"What can I do? I am so fond of jewelry. It is my only weakness. We cannot change our nature."

Then she would wind the pearl necklace round her fingers, make the facets of the crystal gems sparkle, and say:

"Look! Are they not lovely? One would swear they were real."

. . . Sometimes, of an evening, when they were enjoying a tete-a-tete by the fireside, she would place on the tea table the morocco leather box containing the "trash," as Monsieur Lantin called it. She would examine the false gems with a passionate attention, as though they imparted some deep and secret joy; and she often persisted in passing a necklace around her husband's neck, and, laughing heartily, would exclaim: "How droll you look!" Then she would throw herself into his arms, and kiss him affectionately.

One evening, in winter, she had been to the opera, and returned home chilled through and through. The next morning she coughed, and eight days later she died of inflammation of the lungs.

Monsieur Lantin's despair was so great that his hair became white in one month. He wept unceasingly; his heart was broken as he remembered her smile, her voice, every charm of his dead wife.

Time did not assuage his grief. . . . Everything in his wife's room remained as it was during her lifetime; all her furniture, even her clothing, being left as it was on the day of her death. Here he was wont to seclude himself daily and think of her who had been his treasure—the joy of his existence.

But life soon became a struggle. His income, which, in the hands of his wife, covered all household expenses, was now no longer sufficient for his own immediate wants; and he wondered how she could have managed to buy such excellent wine and the rare delicacies which he could no longer procure with his modest resources . . . .

One morning, finding himself without a cent in his pocket, he resolved to sell something, and immediately the thought occurred to him of disposing of his wife's paste jewels, for he cherished in his heart a sort of rancor against these "deceptions," which had always irritated him in the past. The very sight of them spoiled, somewhat, the memory of his lost darling.

To the last days of her life she had continued to make purchases, bringing home new gems almost every evening, and he turned them over some time before finally deciding to sell the heavy necklace, which she seemed to prefer, and which, he thought, ought to be worth about six or seven francs; for it was of very fine workmanship, though only imitation.

He put it in his pocket, and started out in search of what seemed a reliable jeweler's shop. At length he found one, and went in, feeling a little ashamed to expose his misery, and also to offer such a worthless article for sale. . . .

As soon as the proprietor glanced at the necklace, he cried out:

"Ah, parbleu! I know it well; it was bought here."

Monsieur Lantin, greatly disturbed, asked:

"How much is it worth?"

"Well, I sold it for twenty thousand francs. I am willing to take it back for eighteen thousand, when you inform me, according to our legal formality, how it came to be in your possession."

This time, Monsieur Lantin was dumbfounded. He replied:

"But—but—examine it well. Until this moment I was under the impression that it was imitation."

The jeweler asked:

"What is your name, sir?"

"Lantin—I am in the employ of the Minister of the Interior. I live at number sixteen Rue des Martyrs."

The merchant looked through his books, found the entry, and said: "That necklace was sent to Madame Lantin's address, sixteen Rue des Martyrs, July 20, 1876."

The two men looked into each other's eyes—the widower speechless with astonishment; the jeweler scenting a thief. The latter broke the silence.

"Will you leave this necklace here for twenty-four hours?" said he; "I will give you a receipt."

Monsieur Lantin answered hastily: "Yes, certainly." Then, putting the ticket in his pocket, he left the store. . . .

It must have been a present!—a present!—a present, from whom? Why was it given her?

. . . A horrible doubt entered his mind—She? Then, all the other jewels must have been presents, too!

The sun awoke him next morning, and he began to dress slowly to go to the office. It was hard to work after such shocks. He sent a letter to his employer, requesting to be excused. Then he remembered that he had to return to the jeweler's. . . . It was a lovely day; a clear, blue sky smiled on the busy city below. Men of leisure were strolling about with their hands in their pockets.

Monsieur Lantin, observing them, said to himself: "The rich, indeed, are happy. With money it is possible to forget even the deepest sorrow. . . . Oh if I were only rich!"

He perceived that he was hungry, but his pocket was empty. He again remembered the necklace. Eighteen thousand francs! Eighteen thousand francs! What a sum!

He soon arrived in the Rue de la Paix, opposite the jeweler's. Eighteen thousand francs! Twenty times he resolved to go in, but shame kept him back. He was hungry, however—very hungry—and not a cent in his pocket. He decided quickly, ran across the street, in order not to have time for reflection, and rushed into the store.

The proprietor immediately came forward, and politely offered him a chair; the clerks glanced at him knowingly.

"I have made inquiries, Monsieur Lantin," said the jeweler, "and if you are still resolved to dispose of the gems, I am ready to pay you the price I offered."

"Certainly, sir," stammered Monsieur Lantin.

Whereupon the proprietor took from a drawer eighteen large bills, counted, and handed them to Monsieur Lantin, who signed a receipt; and, with trembling hand, put the money into his pocket.

As he was about to leave the store, he turned toward the merchant, who still wore the same knowing smile, and lowering his eyes, said:

"I have—I have other gems, which came from the same source. Will you buy them, also?"

The merchant bowed: "Certainly, sir."

. . . An hour later, he returned with the gems . . . making the sum of one hundred and forty-three thousand francs.

The jeweler remarked, jokingly:

"There was a person who invested all her savings in precious stones."

Monsieur Lantin replied, seriously:

"It is only another way of investing one's money."

That day he lunched at Voisin's, and drank wine worth twenty francs a bottle. Then he hired a carriage and made a tour of the Bois. He gazed at the various turnouts with a kind of disdain, and could hardly refrain from crying out to the occupants:

"I, too, am rich!—I am worth two hundred thousand francs."

For the first time in his life, he was not bored at the theatre, and spent the remainder of the night in a gay frolic.

Six months afterward, he married again. His second wife was a very virtuous woman; but had a violent temper. She caused him much sorrow.

(?) Questions

7. "The False Gems" is an example of which popular nineteenth-century literary movement that reflected contemporary society and was linked to the development of science?

   A. imagism

   B. naturalism

   C. modernism

   D. romanticism

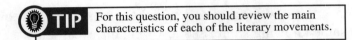 **TIP** For this question, you should review the main characteristics of each of the literary movements.

8. As used in the passage, the phrase "One would swear they were real" is an example of what literary device?

    A. hyperbole

    B. symbolism

    C. personification

    D. foreshadowing

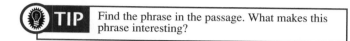 Find the phrase in the passage. What makes this phrase interesting?

9. Which word **best** describes Monsieur Lantin's tone in paragraph 28?

    A. remorseful

    B. bewildered

    C. defensive

    D. sarcastic

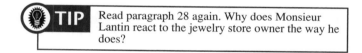 Read paragraph 28 again. Why does Monsieur Lantin react to the jewelry store owner the way he does?

10. This passage illustrates which theme from American literature?

    A. Money can't buy happiness.

    B. Opposites attract each other.

    C. Be careful what you wish for.

    D. Don't judge a book by its cover.

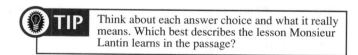 Think about each answer choice and what it really means. Which best describes the lesson Monsieur Lantin learns in the passage?

Passage 4

Read the following passage. Then answer the questions that follow. Use the Tip underneath each question to help you choose the correct answer. When you finish, read the answer explanations at the end of this chapter.

Twins

"Vanessa, can you answer the question?"

My head snaps up from the notebook I've been doodling in. A picture of a strong, black stallion fills the page where my notes should be. My history teacher, Mrs. Vasquez, stares at me intently, anticipating my answer. I wrack my brain, trying to figure out what we've been discussing for the past half an hour. This semester's unit, unfortunately, has been all about the Revolutionary War, but any knowledge of today's lesson eludes me.

I fidget nervously with my pencil as I desperately try to think of something clever to say. After a few moments, I decide that it's time to admit defeat.

"I'm sorry, could you repeat the question?"

Again, Mrs. Vasquez asks for the date of the Boston Tea Party, hoping someone a little more attentive will volunteer an answer. A hand quickly shoots up in the front row and our teacher calls on a student that is, obviously, more prepared than I am.

"1773," says a student in a tone of supreme confidence.

"Very good, Victor. It's too bad your sister doesn't share your aptitude for remembering dates."

I cringe at her words and feel my face redden as a few students chuckle. Before I have an opportunity to keel over and die from embarrassment, the bell rings, signaling the end of a less-than-enlightening academic session. I sigh as I fight my way toward my locker through the throng of students who filter into the halls.

I try not to make a habit of daydreaming in class. It's just that I don't find the Revolutionary War all that stimulating. During most of fifth-period history, I either draw or stare out the window at the courtyard while Mrs. Vasquez drones on and on about Paul Revere, the British, and the battle of Bunker Hill. The 1700s just don't pique my interest as much as a lesson on abstract art might.

As I try to repress any memory of the previous class, my twin brother approaches me. The horde that has invaded the halls of West Palm Beach High School seems to part, allowing Victor to make his way effortlessly whereas I was nearly crushed by several upperclassmen. Of course, Victor's extremely popular, a star athlete, and one of the most intelligent people I know. It's little wonder that the student body would make way for the big man on campus.

His perfection is a little hard to deal with sometimes. Albeit, I have a decent grade-point average and a group of steadfast friends, but I'm not quite as beloved as Victor. Usually, I'm okay with this.

However, I tend to find comments like the one Mrs. Vasquez made this morning especially irksome. People think that just because Victor and I are twins that they can constantly compare us to one another. Why can't they recognize the fact that we're individuals with our own interests, flaws, and strengths?

Of course, like any brother and sister, we have a few similarities. We both like those campy horror movies that air late at night on the science fiction network and we like to go surfing in the early morning while all the tourists are still asleep in their overpriced hotel rooms. We both detest strawberry ice cream and those ridiculous bumper stickers that tell you to honk if you love scuba diving or Jack Russell terriers. Nevertheless, the similarities seem to end there. Victor is the ambitious, outgoing one who is never home on a Saturday night, and I'm the quiet, introspective one who'd rather paint a masterpiece . . . or, at least, attempt to paint a masterpiece.

Victor smiles while I shove my history textbook into my already cramped locker. He kindly informs me that I'd better come up with stringent study schedule if I plan on passing Mrs. Vasquez's midterm exam next week.

Laughing wryly, I ask him if he really thinks he's being witty.

Victor shrugs his shoulders and then offers his academic assistance this weekend, that is after he makes some crucial appearances at all the hippest places.

I tell him I'll think about it as the bell rings, causing students to scurry to their next classes.

Later that night, after completing my homework, I decide to work on a painting I'd started earlier in the week. The canvas is almost completely blank, except for the outline of an old, warped-looking tree. While I rummage through my art supplies, tearing apart the box as I search for a particular shade of green, I hear the sound of the front door opening. It must be my parents, home from yet another one of my brother's football games. As I start shading in a few leaves, the noise from downstairs increases and becomes rather raucous, forcing me to go investigate the source of all the commotion.

Downstairs I find my parents, brother, and a dozen of his teammates. They admonish me for missing the most incredible game ever during which Victor scored the winning touch-down, ensuring the team a trip to the play-offs. My dad orders a few celebratory pizzas and my mom dashes to the convenience store to pick up some soda. I offer Victor and his friends my most enthusiastic congratulations, but I'm fairly certain that a twinge of annoyance is visible in my eyes. I can't help but feel a little slighted by my parents' reaction to my brother's big night. I highly doubt that they'd be throwing me an impromptu pizza party for a dozen of my friends on a school night if I'd won first place in an art exhibition. They would be proud of me and try to do something special, like make my favorite meal, but I don't think they would be as elated about a prize-winning watercolor as they are about a game-winning play. Despite feeling slightly miffed, I help my dad empty bags of chips and pretzels into plastic bowls as the boys exchange exuberant high-fives.

After everyone's gone home and we've finished helping my parents tidy up, Victor and I watch TV in the den. Just before the show we're watching comes back from a commercial break, our dad storms into the room. He's mad at me because I forgot to take out the trash and now we've missed the weekly pickup. I tell him I'm sorry that I forgot, but he's pretty aggravated and complains that he'll have to take it all to the waste station after work tomorrow. I apologize again, but it doesn't seem to be enough.

"Victor remembered to put the trash out last week when it was his turn, why couldn't you?" he asks. At that moment, something inside me snaps. "Well, we all can't be perfect like Victor," I shriek before making a mad dash for my room.

I slam the door loudly, hoping to take some of my frustration out on the wooden frame. It seems to shake the entire house, but I could really care less. I flop down on my bed and feel sorry for myself. I usually don't let this sort of thing bother me, but today has been too much. It's like everywhere I go all I hear about is how studious, responsible, and generally wonderful my brother is. If you ask me, it's enough to make any girl have a bit of a hysterical breakdown.

After spending about fifteen minutes wallowing in self-pity, I hear a knock on my door. I tell whomever it is to go away, but the knocking persists. After a third attempt at gaining admittance, the person ignores my pleas to be left alone and lets himself in. It's Victor. I groan and tell him I want to be left alone. He sits on the edge of my bed and asks me why I'm so upset.

I laugh a little bitterly. "Isn't it obvious?"

"Not really. Why don't you try explaining it to me," he replies. But how do I do that? It doesn't seem fair to tell him that I'm irrationally jealous of the admiration people shower him with on a daily basis. It's not right to fault him simply because he's smart and talented. Of course, my brain isn't working in the most logical manner at the moment and I tell him how I truly feel.

"I'm upset because it seems like you can do no wrong, and everyone seems to think I'm a complete failure. The bad twin!" I exclaim.

Victor laughs loudly at this and then looks at me like some alien life form has taken possession of my body. "Are you crazy?"

"First there was Mrs. Vasquez's remark this morning, then there was the party, and finally Dad yelling at me . . . they all think you're perfect and that I don't measure up."

"Come on, Vanessa. I make just as many mistakes as you do." Victor explains that just today he'd forgotten to compose an original haiku for English class and received an incomplete. He also admits to missing the ball in the first half of tonight's game and says if he hadn't made that final play, his football coach would have been furious and blamed Victor for losing the game. And, he reminds me, that Dad was more than a little upset last week when Victor forgot to fill up his car after borrowing it and Dad ran out of gas on his way to work the next morning.

I consider all of this for a few moments. It was true that our dad had been pretty irate about the whole car situation, but I still feel like everyone is comparing the two of us. After I inform Victor of this, he just laughs again.

"I get compared to you all the time, you know. I hate going to art class now because all Mr. Johnson talks about is how talented my sister is and how he can't believe that one twin got all the artistic ability and the other can barely draw a stick figure." My mouth gapes open as Victor continues.

"He's right though—you're a really amazing artist. I've always been a little jealous of your talent. I can't even draw a straight line." My infallible brother is jealous of me? I stare at him a little stunned.

"The way I see it, everyone's always going to compare us. The best we can do is appreciate our differences," he wisely observes.

I give him a smile and he puts his arm around my shoulder. "Of course, you do know that if you ever mention this conversation to anyone I'll have to disavow any knowledge of it," Victor says. I laugh a little and start to feel better than I have all day.

⑦ Questions

11. Which of the following conclusions can logically be drawn from the passage?

   A. Vanessa does better in art class than anyone else in school.

   B. Victor has lost many more football games than he has won.

   C. Vanessa has a much better memory than her brother Victor.

   D. Victor is not as exceptional in his classes as Vanessa thinks.

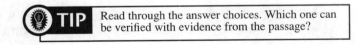

TIP Read through the answer choices. Which one can be verified with evidence from the passage?

12. What is the **most likely** reason that people compare Vanessa and Victor?

   A. They are twins.

   B. He is an athlete.

   C. She is an artist.

   D. They are alike.

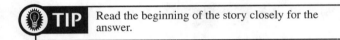

TIP Read the beginning of the story closely for the answer.

13. In the passage, Vanessa characterizes her family to suggest that

    A. she doesn't admire Victor.

    B. her dad likes Victor more.

    C. she has no good qualities.

    D. her brother has no faults.

TIP Scan the passage for places where Vanessa describes the members of her family.

14. As used by the narrator, the phrase "It's enough to make any girl have a bit of a hysterical breakdown" is an example of which literary device?

    A. irony

    B. hyperbole

    C. personification

    D. foreshadowing

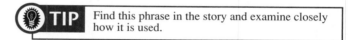

TIP Find this phrase in the story and examine closely how it is used.

 # Answers

1. B

   The point of view of this passage is very close to Babette. The author describes how she peeks excitedly at the figs each day only to walk away saddened; this makes it clear that she is excited about leaving soon.

2. A

   The story implies that patience is something that is learned with age. Waiting is harder for the young. Answer choice A is the best answer.

3. C

   The ripening of the figs coincides with the beginning of summer according to the details revealed in the story. None of the other answer choices are backed up by evidence in the text. Answer choice C is correct.

4. C

   The narrator presents the main idea of the passage—that the swing was one of her favorite places to think. Then, she tells anecdotes from the past.

5. B

   The narrator uses the phrase "pendulum-like motion" to describe the movement of a swing. Like the pendulum on a clock, the swing simply moves back and forth.

6. D

   The narrator chose these words as a sort of metaphor for the progression of life. As a child, her grandfather comforted and entertained her, but as she got older, she had to do things for herself.

7. B

   "The False Gems" is an example of naturalism. In literature, naturalism is a believeable everyday reality.

8. D

   The phrase is interesting because it foreshadows the end of the story.

9. B

   Until he arrives at the jewelry store, Monsieur Lantin thinks the jewels are imitations. When the owner offers him a lot of money for them, he realizes they are real and he is shocked.

10. A

At the end of the passage, Monsieur Lantin thinks he will be much easier now that he is rich; however, the new wife he chooses makes him miserable.

11. D

Although all of the answer choices are possible, the only one backed up by evidence in the text is that Victor doesn't do as well in his classes as Vanessa thinks he does. Victor says that he doesn't do very well in his art class.

12. A

Early in the story Vanessa explains that people always compare the two siblings because they are twins.

13. D

Through the beginning of the story, Vanessa characterizes her brother as being flawless and perfect.

14. B

This statement by the narrator is an exaggeration, or an example of hyperbole.

Chapter 6
Elements of Nonfiction

Georgia Performance Standards

ELAALRL1 The student demonstrates comprehension by identifying evidence (e.g., diction, imagery, point of view, figurative language, symbolism, plot events, and main ideas) in a variety of texts representative of different genres (e.g., poetry, prose [short story, novel, essay, editorial, biography], and drama) and using this evidence as the basis for interpretation.

ELAALRL1.nonfiction. The student identifies, analyzes, and applies knowledge of the purpose, structure, and elements of nonfiction and/or informational materials and provides evidence from the text to support understanding; the student

a. analyzes and explains the structures and elements of nonfiction works of American literature such as letters, journals and diaries, speeches, and essays;

b. analyzes and evaluates the logic and use of evidence in an author's argument;

c. analyzes, evaluates, and applies knowledge of the ways authors use language, style, syntax, and rhetorical strategies for specific purposes in nonfiction works.

Nonfiction Literature

In Chapter 5, you learned about the elements of fiction. You can use that knowledge when reading novels, poetry, short stories, or works of drama. However, there is also a wide range of writings that don't fit into the fiction category. In order to get the most out of these kinds of works, you need to know the elements of nonfiction.

Like fiction, nonfiction comes in a variety of forms. The questions on the Georgia High School Graduation Test (GHSGT) may require you to analyze different types of nonfiction. These are some of the major varieties of nonfiction writing:

- **Letters:** written communication between people (often friends or family members) that usually exchanges personal opinions, information, and news of current events. Friendly letters are often written to friends and family, while business letters are written to professionals and formal invitations of acceptance are written to organizations or professionals within those organizations

- **Journals and diaries:** an author's personal record of events, ideas, and feelings, which are usually added to on a regular basis

- **Essays:** short works of literature that typically deal with a single topic and present the personal views of the writer, which are sometimes backed up with researched facts

- **Speeches:** writings that are intended to be read in public, often with the intent of persuading others or gathering support of a cause or belief

Evidence and Logic

The GHSGT will test your knowledge of nonfiction in several ways. For example, questions about a persuasive nonfiction passage may ask you to evaluate an author's argument. How does the author use proof, or **evidence**, to support his or her claims or conclusions? Do the author's arguments and evidence make sense? A **logical** argument will be based on reasoning—a clear, careful progression of ideas. Here are some arguments and some logical evidence that helps support the arguments:

Argument	Logical Evidence
Nancy Curry is the best candidate for our city's mayor.	1. Nancy Curry spent four years as a successful city council member. 2. She has lived in our city for thirty years and knows most of its residents. 3. She worked with our current mayor and learned about city governance.
Uniforms should be mandatory for all public school students.	1. School uniforms can cost less than a wardrobe of "street clothing." 2. School uniforms help students and faculty identify trespassers on school property. 3. Studies have shown that standardized clothing reduces student rivalry.

Author's Purpose

Writers often use nonfiction compositions to inform or persuade their readers. In order to meet these purposes, writers have to construct their nonfiction works carefully, making many decisions to enhance their writing's effectiveness. The GHSGT will test your ability to analyze and evaluate how authors choose to construct their nonfiction writings, and for what purpose they have chosen to do so. In order to determine an author's purpose for writing, you may be asked to evaluate these factors:

- **Language:** the words chosen by the author, and the way he or she arranges them

- **Style:** the "feel" of the writing, as conveyed by the author's tone, rhythm, and attitude toward the subject and reader

- **Syntax:** the way the author observes the rules of grammar and combines words into grammatical sentences

- **Rhetorical strategies:** the ways in which an author can present an argument

An author can use a wide range of rhetorical strategies to put forth arguments or other important ideas. Some of these strategies may include using imagery (appeals to the reader's senses) or themes (references to broad concepts or beliefs). An author might organize a nonfiction piece using counterpoints (contrasting ideas), analogies or metaphors (comparisons), or repetition (repeating words or phrases for emphasis).

Passage 1

Read the following selection. Then answer the questions that follow. Use the Tip underneath each question to help you choose the correct answer. When you finish, read the answer explanations at the end of this chapter.

Curious Crop Circles

1   Imagine, for a moment, that you're a farmer. One morning you awaken to find a large circular pattern in the middle of your fields. Where rows of wheat, soy, or corn stood tall just yesterday, there is now a perfectly shaped circle. For many farmers around the world, this is a baffling reality. This strange phenomenon is known as crop circles and they are characterized by the symmetrical flattening of crops into a geometric pattern, usually occurring overnight when there are no witnesses. The formations generally appear starting in late spring until early autumn, with most circles being discovered during the summer months. The United Kingdom has had the largest number of crop circles over the years, but countries like the United States, Germany, Canada, and The Netherlands have reported an increase in incidents since the late twentieth century.

2   Crop circles first garnered international attention in the media during the early 1980s when a series of circles were discovered in southern England. However, many argue that these circles have been reported since the early seventeenth century. A tale dating back to

1678 tells of a farmer who refused to pay a laborer to mow the farmer's field. That night, the field appeared to be on fire. When the farmer went to inspect his crops the following morning, instead of finding charred remains, he discovered that the field had indeed been mowed—by whom or what he couldn't say. While many dispute the validity of this early incident, others note that farmers have been reporting crop circles for generations.

3   Of course, the real mystery is who or what is behind the creation of these circles in the middle of the night. Theories explaining the existence of crop circles range from the mundane to the supernatural. Many feel that most crop circles are nothing but elaborate hoaxes perpetrated by people who have nothing better to do with their time or who are looking for their fifteen minutes of fame.

4   Two of the most famous hoaxers were discovered in England. In 1991, Doug Bower and Dave Chorley claimed that they had been staging crop circles for nearly fifteen years, creating over two hundred circles. The men said they would sneak into the fields at night using a wooden plank tied to some string to flatten the crops into circles while the owners of the field were asleep. While Bower and Chorley may have been telling the truth, this does not account for the more than two thousand other circles that were reported around the country during the time they were working.

5   Today, the debate over hoaxing continues. Professional circle-makers have appeared on numerous television programs, trying to prove that crop circles, even the extremely complex ones, are man-made. Circle-makers have created formations for everything from music videos to movies, like the 2002 hit *Signs*. There are even several businesses that use computer technology to create circle advertisements in fields where airplane passengers are most likely to spot them.

6   Still, crop circle researchers note several key differences between artificial and what they call authentic crop circles. First, researchers note that when an artificial pattern is formed, there is usually evidence of a human presence left behind, like footprints in the soil or impressions from the tools that were used. Second, when a genuine formation is found, there are sometimes unexplainable effects on the environment that do not occur when a circle is the work of tricksters.

7   One especially interesting fact that researchers point out is that crops that are particularly unyielding, like canola plants, tend to snap when they are bent by the tools that many hoaxers use, whereas these same crops inexplicably bend in "legitimate" formations. Other important differences that researchers have noted between what they feel are real crop circles and hoaxes are cellular changes in plants, changes in a plant's seeds, and dehydrated soil in genuine cases.

8   The most popular, and the most controversial, idea behind the cause of crop circles is that they are the work of extraterrestrial life forms trying to make contact with human beings. Proponents of this idea believe that the formations must be created by an intelligent life form and that the circles are far too intricate for even a small team of humans to create overnight

without being caught. To support this claim, many people point to other strange phenomena that sometimes accompany crop circles as evidence of an alien presence. These reports include seeing balls of light and hearing unusual sounds in the areas where the circles are later discovered. Some believe that this theory might also explain the curious effect that some circles have on plants, but so far there is not enough conclusive evidence to link crop circles to an otherworldly force.

9   The search for a more terrestrial answer to the cause of crop circles continues. Some scientists believe that the earth itself is the cause of these mysterious events. One argument is that a shift in the earth's electromagnetic field would be enough to flatten crops without breaking them. Another idea is that changes in the planet's weather patterns over the last few centuries could be the source of crop circles. There are several other theories that conclude that crop circles are probably more natural than supernatural.

10   While some crop circle cases are proved to be nothing more than mere pranks, others are not so easy to dismiss. Until there is a clear-cut explanation for the phenomenon, it's likely that these mysterious formations will continue to fascinate researchers and regular people worldwide for some time to come.

ⓠ Questions

1. The author asks the reader to imagine being a farmer who finds a crop circle in order to show readers that

    A. they would not be good farmers.

    B. only farmers can see crop circles.

    C. crop circles are very surprising.

    D. crop circles are made by farmers.

 TIP Think about your reaction when you first read this. If you imagined being a farmer finding a crop circle in a field, what effect did that image have on you? Did it help you find meaning in the passage?

2. The author described crop circles being made

   for everything from music videos to movies, like the 2002 hit *Signs*.

   The most likely reason the author chose these words would be to

   A. indicate that many movies feature crop circles.

   B. show that crop circles are well-known symbols.

   C. demonstrate how fake crop circles are made.

   D. suggest that all crop circles are made by experts.

 Read this excerpt carefully. The author says that crop circles have been made for music videos and movies, including a recent, popular movie. What point is the author probably trying to make?

3. Which of these facts from the passage would be most relevant to use in a presentation about crop circles and extraterrestrial life?

   A. Doug Bower and Dave Chorley claimed that they had been staging crop circles for nearly fifteen years.

   B. One argument is that a shift in the earth's electromagnetic field would be enough to flatten crops without breaking them.

   C. Reports include seeing balls of light and hearing unusual sounds in the areas where the circles are later discovered.

   D. A tale dating back to 1678 tells of a farmer who refused to pay a laborer to mow the farmer's field.

 Read over each of these facts and think about what you learned in the passage. If you were doing a presentation on crop circles and extraterrestrial life, which of these facts would provide the most information?

Passage 2

Read the following selection. Then answer the questions that follow. Use the Tip underneath each question to help you choose the correct answer. When you finish, read the answer explanations at the end of this chapter.

Glorytown Gazette

Letters to the Editor

American Aid Essential for First-Rate Foreign Relations

To the Editor:

1 I am writing in response to a letter in yesterday's newspaper. In the letter, Edwin Stanton stated that the United States should not give financial aid to foreign countries. Mr. Stanton feels that our government should not give away its money, no matter what the cause. He stated that "each nation should be responsible for standing on its own two feet," and that "America should not help poor people of other nations when there is so much poverty at home." While I do believe that a couple of the points in Mr. Stanton's letter are good ones, most are based on misconceptions. I hope that most of my fellow citizens don't share his views. If they do, we may someday be in trouble and find ourselves with nowhere to turn.

2 Our government often hands out aid to other countries to help these countries become democracies. It seems that nations under a dictatorship are far less likely to conduct positive foreign relations with the United States than those with a democratic government. By providing money—along with other types of aid—to foreign countries, America can make peace with them. This helps create political and military friendships that may help us in the future. By aiding others, we aid ourselves as well.

3 I don't think that Mr. Stanton understands the figures in this debate, either. America spends less than one percent of its money on foreign aid. This is hardly an enormous waste of taxpayer dollars. Many other countries, such as Japan and Sweden, spend much more on foreign aid. Furthermore, many other countries have offered help to *us* in times of need. Cuba and Venezuela have offered even though our relationship with them has been strained.

4 I just hope that people who read Mr. Stanton's letter think about these points as well, and not accept his ideas. If we all thought this way, the world would never change.

Kat McClanahan

Glorytown, USA

? Questions

4. This passage is an example of a persuasive letter because of its

    A. presentation of a clear argument.

    B. explanation of a certain viewpoint.

    C. use of statistics and other facts.

    D. quoting of another, earlier writer.

     Think about what you know about persuasive letters. Then, think of how this passage fits the description of a persuasive letter.

5. Which assertion is **best** supported by the evidence in the passage?

    A. We should give help because we might need help.

    B. We should not help countries that do not help us.

    C. Foreign aid represents a large portion of our budget.

    D. Most people share Mr. Stanton's views on foreign aid.

     Read over these assertions carefully. Think back to the information in the passage. Which assertion is most supported by evidence?

6. The **most likely** reason the author wrote this passage was to

    A. provide further support to Mr. Stanton's claims.

    B. encourage people to donate to charitable causes.

    C. dispute the argument put forth by another writer.

    D. tell people America should decrease foreign aid.

     Skim over the passage you've just read. Think about the information it contains. What effect did this information have on you? Why did the author probably write this passage?

7. Throughout the passage, Kat McClanahan refutes Mr. Stanton's argument by

    A. listing countries to which America has given aid.

    B. showing that foreign aid is a waste of taxpayer money.

    C. showing how other countries have offered America money.

    D. suggesting that foreign aid builds good relationships.

     Find the parts in the passage in which Ms. McClanahan refutes Mr. Stanton's argument. What main reason does she give readers to accept her ideas over Mr. Stanton's?

Passage 3

Read the following selection. Then answer the questions that follow. Use the Tip underneath each question to help you choose the correct answer. When you finish, read the answer explanations at the end of this chapter.

Safe at Sixteen? Why We Should Raise the Legal Driving Age
by Eliot Golden

1   To many teens, turning sixteen is a rite of passage. In most states, this is the age when young people can apply for a driver's license. Teens see this as the beginning of freedom and independence. They think it is a time to enjoy being young and carefree. Though many teens feel excited about being able to drive, many adults feel that this is a dangerous and sometimes deadly time for young drivers. Their fears are often confirmed by some scary statistics. Studies show that young drivers are more likely to speed, run red lights, and drive recklessly than more mature, experienced drivers.

2   Many experts agree that this kind of behavior accounts for the thousands of teens killed every year in automobile accidents. In fact, according to the National Center for Injury Prevention and Control, teens are four times more likely to crash than older drivers. This has caused many to question what can be done to keep teen drivers safe.

3   A growing number of people feel that the only way to truly prevent tragedy is to raise the legal driving age. Most teens, and even some parents, scoff at this idea. However, many people feel that this is necessary. Some of our nation's lawmakers agree. A number of states have already raised the minimum age a teen must be to acquire a full, unrestricted license. This means that many young drivers can only drive with a licensed adult in the car. These states use graduated licensing programs that put limitations on young drivers. The programs restrict teens from driving late at night or carrying other teenage passengers until they have logged a certain number of hours driving under the supervision of a parent or guardian. Safety experts point out that more supervised experience makes safer drivers and reduces the risk of fatal accidents among teens. But are these programs doing enough to keep kids safe?

4   Researchers also note that maturity plays a major role in safety on the roads. Many young drivers are overconfident in their abilities. They don't think about the risks associated with getting behind the wheel. Studies show that out of all age groups, teens are the most likely to drive while under the influence of alcohol or drugs. They are also the most likely to drive without wearing a seat belt and underestimate the dangers of hazardous road

conditions. Some argue that making mature decisions about driving is something that can only come with age. These people feel that the number of hours they spend practicing doesn't matter.

5   Keeping all of this in mind, the only logical and responsible solution to this problem is to raise the legal driving age. Many teens will argue that their freedom is being taken from them. Many parents might be inconvenienced by having to drive their kids to school, work, or practice. But the alternative is far worse! Turning sixteen is an important milestone in any young person's life, but it doesn't necessarily mean that he or she is ready to drive. By raising the legal driving age and giving teens more time and experience behind the wheel, we can help make sure that turning seventeen, eighteen, and nineteen is just as exciting and safe for teens.

? Questions

8. The end of the first paragraph helps to create a tone that is

    A. uplifting.

    B. disturbing.

    C. bitter.

    D. majestic.

 Think about the way the first paragraph started. How has the tone changed by the time you finish the final sentence? How does the end of the paragraph set the tone for the rest of the passage?

9. According to this author, how are teenage drivers unlike older drivers?

    A. Teens are four times more likely to be involved in car crashes.

    B. Teens are almost always under the influence while driving.

    C. Teens know to use caution when they get behind the wheel.

    D. Teens are mature enough to handle most dangerous situations.

 Take another look at the second paragraph. The author explains the differences between teenage drivers and older drivers. Consider each option before choosing an answer.

10. Which **best** describes the way in which the passage is structured?

    A. a sequence of events

    B. a problem followed by a solution

    C. a claim followed by anecdotes

    D. a listing of statistics

 TIP Look back to the passage. Note what happens in the beginning, middle, and end of the passage. Decide what "path" the author takes to make his points.

11. In the third paragraph, the author gives examples to suggest that

    A. teens feel they are having their freedoms taken away.

    B. the driving rules in use now are perfectly sufficient.

    C. early efforts to prepare teens for driving aren't enough.

    D. driving is becoming more dangerous every year.

 TIP Go back and reread the third paragraph of the essay. What is the author trying to communicate to the reader in this paragraph? Choose your answer carefully.

Passage 4

Read the following passage. Then answer the questions that follow. Use the Tip underneath each question to help you choose the correct answer. When you finish, read the answer explanations at the end of this chapter.

Daydreams Save the Day
by Ricardo Sanchez

1   Many students have gotten in trouble for daydreaming in class. It's not a good idea to be thinking about your new skateboard or your weekend plans when you should be learning algebra! It's rude to the instructor, and you might not learn what you need to know. However, many scientists agree that daydreaming itself isn't a bad thing at all. In fact, daydreams can make your life happier and healthier in numerous ways.

2   Some psychologists believe that the average person daydreams for many hours each day. Critics of daydreaming say that this is a dreadful waste of time. Daydreaming usually doesn't result in any obvious progress; it's usually seen as something that keeps people from making progress. This is not really the case, however. Sometimes daydreaming can help people sort out their minds and get their ideas in order so that they can think and behave a lot more effectively. Their daydreams can make them more productive workers or students, and make future progress easier.

3   There are many negative stereotypes about daydreamers, such as that they are lazy and that they shirk responsibilities. While this can be true, it's definitely not always true. Sometimes daydreams actually give people a goal to work toward. For instance, a writer might daydream about seeing his or her book in print, and this image builds determination to keep on writing. In this way, daydreams can be a method of visualizing success in the future. Some athletes use "positive thinking" visualization while practicing. By thinking about their challenges and imagining success in the end, they tend to perform much better than athletes who haven't prepared their minds.

4   A third criticism of daydreams is that too much daydreaming can make people unhappy. Of course, if a person daydreams *all day*, he or she will probably lose track of the events of real life! He or she might start to "live in the past" or in some unrealistic dream world. But for people who do a regular amount of daydreaming, the practice can make them happier. This can happen in many ways.

5   For one, daydreaming allows the mind to relax. Especially in stressful times, giving your mind a break is a great idea. Taking a "mini-vacation" by daydreaming can make a person's brain feel energized and refreshed. These vacations are also great for overcoming boredom. Excessive boredom can have negative effects on people and cause them to feel gloomy and tired. A little daydreaming here and there can relieve the nasty effects of boredom.

6   Many psychologists think that daydreams can also help remove fear and conflict from our lives. Just like athletes who use daydreams to prepare for events, other people can use them to learn to deal with themselves and others. If two people aren't getting along they might be able to daydream, or visualize, ways in which they could reconcile. They might even be able to use daydreams to imagine the others' points-of-view and find similarities or shared interests between themselves and others. Daydreaming can help us expand our minds, and that helps us find new ways to get along with others.

7   In much the same way, people can use daydreams to ease, and even conquer, their fears. For example, if a person has a powerful fear, or phobia, of heights, he or she might imagine safely climbing higher and higher on a hill. This can prepare the person to remain calm while climbing the hill. "Positive thinking" daydreams can strengthen a person's courage considerably. Many people have used this simple technique to conquer their phobias.

8   There are many good kinds of daydreaming that help people improve their lives. However, bad types of daydreaming exist as well. One of these is "negative daydreaming," which occurs most frequently in the behavior we know as "worrying." Some people get caught up in worries, and spend their days nervously picturing all sorts of frightening and embarrassing events. Worries can have a terrible effect on people's lives. Sometimes worries can keep people awake all night; other times worries and stress can weaken the body, causing people to get sick more easily.

9   One of the best ways to combat negative daydreams like worrying is to counter them with "positive daydreams." Instead of worrying, a person can take a more relaxed look at his or her problems. He or she can reflect on the past and imagine some possibilities of the future, and then try to decide how to handle these thoughts. By using positive daydreams and visualizations, you may well be able to overcome many kinds of negative thoughts and feelings.

10   Daydreams play an important role in our daily lives, a role that not many people stop to consider. Good daydreams can make us healthy and happy, and bad daydreams can do just the opposite. But just remember—no daydreams are good daydreams in algebra class!

(?) Questions

12. In the passage, the author puts several words and terms in quotation marks in order to

    A. show that they are often misunderstood.

    B. show that they are quoted from a source.

    C. suggest that they could be ignored by readers.

    D. indicate psychological terminology.

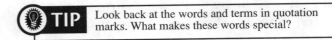

TIP Look back at the words and terms in quotation marks. What makes these words special?

13. The author wrote that it's a bad idea to daydream about

    your new skateboard or your weekend plans when you should be learning algebra!

    The **most likely** reason the author chose these words would be to

    A. demonstrate that daydreams have a positive effect.

    B. imply that only young people have daydreams.

    C. suggest that people only have happy daydreams.

    D. explain that daydreams may interfere in people's lives.

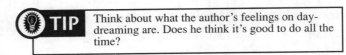

TIP Think about what the author's feelings on daydreaming are. Does he think it's good to do all the time?

14. What is an example of negative daydreaming, according to this author?

    A. visualizing the completion of a project before it's done

    B. losing track of the present while thinking of the past

    C. imagining ways to conquer a fear or worry

    D. allowing your mind to wander for a few minutes

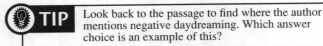

TIP Look back to the passage to find where the author mentions negative daydreaming. Which answer choice is an example of this?

✔ Answers

1. C

   When the author asks you to imagine being a farmer who finds a crop circle, the author wants to show you how surprising crop circles can be. If you were a farmer, you might expect many things to happen in a day, but finding a pattern in your fields would probably not be one of them.

2. B

   These words do not explain how experts make crop circles or how many movies feature crop circles. Instead, by giving some brief examples of how crop circles are portrayed in popular media, the author shows that crop circles are a well-known symbol in our society.

3. C

   Unusual sounds and balls of light being linked to crop circles can hint at the circles' possible extraterrestrial origins. In a presentation on that topic, this fact would be the most helpful. The other facts pertain to other, less relevant topics.

4. A

   While each of these descriptions does apply to the passage, answer choice A in particular defines what makes the passage a persuasive letter. You've already learned that persuasive passages make an argument, which this passage does.

5. A

   In the letter, the author says that giving foreign aid can help America by building friendships. The new friends, in turn, may help America later. In other words, America should give assistance to other countries now in case America requires assistance in the future.

6. C

   The author of this letter is primarily concerned with disputing the argument made earlier by Mr. Stanton. The author begins the letter by quoting Mr. Stanton and summarizing his ideas. Then, the author goes on to argue against many of these ideas.

7. D

   Kat McClanahan's main argument against Mr. Stanton's ideas is that America's foreign aid builds good relationships with other countries. Answer choice B is contrary to her argument. Answer choice A was not included in the letter, and choice C was not the most important point in the letter. Answer choice D is best.

8. B

The first paragraph starts by talking about teenage driving in a positive way, but then suddenly brings out "scary statistics." This serves to create a disturbing tone that brings attention to the severity of the dangers.

9. A

In the second paragraph, the author directly states that, according to the National Center for Injury Prevention and Control, "teens are four times more likely to crash than older drivers."

10. B

The author of this passage does not work much with anecdotes, events, or statistics. However, he does open the passage with a problem (dangerous teenage driving) and work his way toward a possible solution (restricting teenage driving).

11. C

The author does not address the points given in answer choices A or D. The point in choice B, namely that current laws are sufficient, is contrary to the author's argument. In paragraph 3, the author points out that early efforts to curb teenage driving problems were a good start, but they weren't good enough.

12. D

The author puts in quotation marks words that relate to psychology. He does this because these are terms that he realizes might not be clear to the reader.

13. D

Although most of the passage is about the benefits of daydreaming, the author acknowledges some bad things about it, too. This excerpt from the first paragraph shows that students may daydream while they should be learning classroom topics. This kind of daydreaming can have negative effects.

14. B

Answer choices A, C, and D contain examples of some positive applications of daydreaming. Only choice B presents a negative one. The author warns people against losing track of reality due to excessive daydreaming.

Chapter 7

Poetry

Georgia Performance Standards

ELAALRL1 The student demonstrates comprehension by identifying evidence (e.g., diction, imagery, point of view, figurative language, symbolism, plot events, and main ideas) in a variety of texts representative of different genres (e.g., poetry, prose [short story, novel, essay, editorial, biography], and drama) and using this evidence as the basis for interpretation.

ELAALRL1.poetry. The student identifies and analyzes elements of poetry from various periods of American literature and provides evidence from the text to support understanding; the student

  a. identifies, responds to, and analyzes the effects of diction, tone, mood, syntax, sound, form, figurative language, and structure of poems as these elements relate to meaning:

   i. **Sound:** alliteration, end rhyme, slant rhyme, internal rhyme, consonance, assonance

   ii. **Form:** fixed and free, lyric, ballad, sonnet, narrative poem, blank verse

   iii. **Figurative language:** personification, imagery, metaphor, conceit, simile, metonymy, synecdoche, hyperbole, symbolism, allusion

  b. analyzes and evaluates the effects of diction and imagery (e.g., controlling images, figurative language, extended metaphor, understatement, hyperbole, irony, paradox, and tone) as they relate to underlying meaning;

  c. traces the historical development of poetic styles and forms in American literature.

Elements of Poetry

Questions on the Georgia High School Graduation Test (GHSGT) for this standard will be on poetry passages. These questions ask about elements of poetry, such as sound, form, figurative language, and structure.

Questions for this standard might ask you to interpret the meaning of selected lines in a poem. Questions might also ask you about a more specific choice of the poet, for instance, the idea the author conveys by choosing to use a certain word or phrase in a poem. Often, these questions will ask you to choose the poetry technique an author uses to convey a certain point. Others might ask you to identify the features of a specific poetic style, such as romanticism, naturalism, or realism. In some cases, you may have to analyze how a certain element in a poem affects its tone or mood.

You might be asked to identify metaphors or similes in poems, as well as instances of personification, hyperbole, symbolism, or other types of figurative language and literary devices. You might be asked to identify effects of sound, such as alliteration, onomatopoeia, rhyme scheme, consonance, and assonance. Questions on this standard might also ask you to identify the form of a poem, such as ballad, sonnet, or heroic couplet.

Passage 1

Read the following passage. Then answer the questions that follow. Use the Tip below each question to help you choose the correct answer. When you finish, read the answer explanations at the end of this chapter.

A London Thoroughfare. 2 A.M.
by Amy Lowell

1   They have watered the street,

It shines in the glare of lamps,

Cold, white lamps,

And lies

5   Like a slow-moving river,

Barred with silver and black.

Cabs go down it,

One,

And then another,

10   Between them I hear the shuffling of feet.

Tramps doze on the window-ledges,

Night-walkers pass along the sidewalks.

The city is squalid and sinister,

With the silver-barred street in the midst,

15   Slow-moving,

A river leading nowhere.

Opposite my window,

The moon cuts,

Clear and round,

20   Through the plum-coloured night.

She cannot light the city:

It is too bright.

It has white lamps,

And glitters coldly.

25 I stand in the window and watch the moon.

She is thin and lustreless,

But I love her.

I know the moon,

And this is an alien city.

⑦ Questions

1. The point of view in the poem reveals

    A. the narrator's unhappiness with where she lives.

    B. the moon's anger that it cannot penetrate the city lights.

    C. the narrator's urge to join the energetic pace of the city.

    D. the moon's need to comfort an old friend.

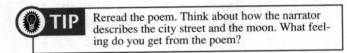
TIP Reread the poem. Think about how the narrator describes the city street and the moon. What feeling do you get from the poem?

2. As used to describe the moon, the phrase "She is thin and lustreless" is an example of which literary device?

    A. simile

    B. personification

    C. allusion

    D. metaphor

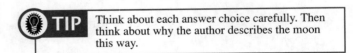
TIP Think about each answer choice carefully. Then think about why the author describes the moon this way.

3. Throughout the poem, Lowell characterizes the city street to suggest that

    A. many people enjoy the sounds of the city at night.

    B. there's nowhere she'd rather be than in the city.

    C. the city is crowded with many interesting people.

    D. it's a dangerous and lonely place for someone to live.

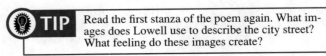
TIP Read the first stanza of the poem again. What images does Lowell use to describe the city street? What feeling do these images create?

Passage 2

Read the following passage. Then answer the questions that follow. Use the Tip underneath each question to help you choose the correct answer. When you finish, read the answer explanations at the end of this chapter.

Excerpt from *Beowulf*

1   You have heard of the Danish Kings

     in the old days and how

     they were great warriors.

     Shield, the son of Sheaf,

5   took many an enemy's chair,

     terrified many a warrior,

     after he was found an orphan.

     He prospered under the sky

     until people everywhere

10 listened when he spoke.

     He was a good king!

(?) Questions

4. As used to describe Shield, the phrase "took many an enemy's chair" is an example of which literary device?

   A. simile

   B. imagery

   C. metonymy

   D. personification

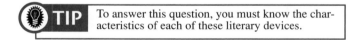 **TIP**   To answer this question, you must know the characteristics of each of these literary devices.

5. Which **best** describes the way in which the poem is structured?

    A. details describing a character

    B. a main idea with anecdotes

    C. comparison and contrast

    D. a problem followed by solutions

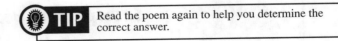 Read the poem again to help you determine the correct answer.

6. This poem is an example of narrative poetry because of its

    A. song-like rhythm.

    B. focus on telling a story.

    C. description of inner feelings.

    D. fixed form and rhyme scheme.

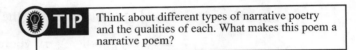 Think about different types of narrative poetry and the qualities of each. What makes this poem a narrative poem?

Passage 3

Read the following passage. Then answer the questions that follow. Use the Tip underneath each question to help you choose the correct answer. When you finish, read the answer explanations at the end of this chapter.

I Wandered Lonely As a Cloud
by William Wordsworth

1   I wandered lonely as a cloud

       That floats on high o'er vales and hills,

       When all at once I saw a crowd,

       A host, of golden daffodils,

5   Beside the lake, beneath the trees

       Fluttering and dancing in the breeze.

       Continuous as the stars that shine

       And twinkle on the Milky Way,

       They stretched in never-ending line

10   Along the margin of a bay:

       Ten thousand saw I at a glance

       Tossing their heads in sprightly dance.

The waves beside them danced, but they

Out-did the sparkling waves in glee:

15 A poet could not but be gay

In such a jocund company:

I gazed—and gazed—but little thought

What wealth the show to me had brought.

For oft, when on my couch I lie

20 In vacant or in pensive mood,

They flash upon that inward eye

Which is the bliss of solitude;

And then my heart with pleasure fills

And dances with the daffodils.

[1807]

❓ Questions

7. This poem is an example of the literary movement romanticism because of its

   A. embrace of diversity, irony, and word play.

   B. focus on inner feelings and images from nature.

   C. description of ordinary people in everyday situations.

   D. attention to facts and reality written in simpler language.

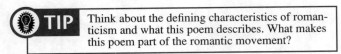

TIP Think about the defining characteristics of romanticism and what this poem describes. What makes this poem part of the romantic movement?

8. Which pair of words from the poem is an example of end rhyme?

   A. *fills* and *daffodils*

   B. *glance* and *eye*

   C. *cloud* and *breeze*

   D. *dance* and *gay*

 TIP Remember that end rhyme occurs when the last syllables of lines in a verse sound the same. Read the poem again and look for the words that end with the same sound.

9. The "flash upon that inward eye" in line 21 is most likely a metaphor for

   A. the view of the daffodils from the sky.

   B. sunlight breaking through the clouds.

   C. the poet's memory of the daffodils.

   D. dancing through a field on a sunny day.

 TIP Read the poem again. When does the "flash" usually occur? How does the "flash" make the poet feel?

10. The phrase "Continuous as the stars that shine / And twinkle on the Milky Way" is a simile for the

   A. amount of flowers the poet sees.

   B. bright color of the daffodils.

   C. height of the waves in the bay.

   D. strength of the breeze through the trees.

 TIP Look for these lines in the poem. Then, try to figure out the comparison the poet is trying to make. To what is the poet comparing the stars in the Milky Way?

Passage 4

Read the following passage. Then answer the questions that follow. Use the Tip underneath each question to help you choose the correct answer. When you finish, read the answer explanations at the end of this chapter.

Ah, Are You Digging on My Grave
Thomas Hardy

"Ah, are you digging on my grave,

My loved one?—planting rue?"

—"No: yesterday he went to wed

One of the brightest wealth has bred.

5   'It cannot hurt her now,' he said,

'That I should not be true.' "

"Then who is digging on my grave,

My nearest dearest kin?"

—"Ah, no: they sit and think, 'What use!

10   What good will planting flowers produce?

No tendance of her mound can loose

Her spirit from Death's gin.' "

"But someone digs upon my grave?

My enemy?—prodding sly?"

15   —"Nay: when she heard you had passed the Gate

That shuts on all flesh soon or late,

She thought you no more worth her hate,

And cares not where you lie.

"Then, who is digging on my grave?

20 Say—since I have not guessed!"

—"O it is I, my mistress dear,

Your little dog, who still lives near,

And much I hope my movements here

Have not disturbed your rest?"

25 "Ah yes! You dig upon my grave . . .

Why flashed it not to me

That one true heart was left behind!

What feeling do we ever find

To equal among human kind

30 A dog's fidelity!"

"Mistress, I dug upon your grave

To bury a bone, in case

I should be hungry near this spot

When passing on my daily trot.

35 I am sorry, but I quite forgot

It was your resting place."

⑦ Questions

11. The author depicts the dog burying a bone on the grave in order to show the dog's

   A. loyalty.

   B. indifference.

   C. remorse.

   D. amusement.

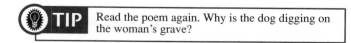

TIP Read the poem again. Why is the dog digging on the woman's grave?

12. The phrase "passed the Gate" is a metaphor for

    A. the time at which a person dies.

    B. the entrance to the graveyard.

    C. the coffin in which the woman is buried.

    D. the people the woman left behind.

 Read the stanza that contains line 15 again. The dog explains that "the Gate . . . shuts on all flesh soon or late." What does this mean?

13. Which line from the poem is an example of alliteration?

    A. "And cares not where you lie"

    B. "No tendance of her mound can loose"

    C. "That one true heart was left behind"

    D. "And much I hope my movements here"

 To answer this question, you must think about what *alliteration* means. Then, consider each answer choice carefully.

14. As used to describe the dog in the poem, the phrase "one true heart" is an example of which literary device?

    A. hyperbole

    B. allusion

    C. symbolism

    D. irony

 Read the last two stanzas of the poem again. Why does the woman think the dog is digging on her grave? What is the dog's real reason for digging?

 Answers

1. **A**

   The narrator seems unhappy with where she is living. This message is conveyed through her descriptions of the city as cold, sinister, and alien.

2. **B**

   By using the word *she*, the poet is personifying the moon to be a woman. She goes on to say "I love her" and points out that the moon is familiar to her, unlike the city street. It is as if the moon is the poet's friend.

3. **D**

   The poet calls the city street squalid, sinister, and cold, and notes that the sidewalks are lined with night-walkers and tramps. These images create a sense that the city street is a dangerous and lonely place.

4. **C**

   Metonymy is a literary device in which the name of one thing is substituted for the name of another thing with which it shares certain attributes. In this case, the generic word *chair* is standing in for more specific words such as *throne* or *kingdom*. It's the poet's way of saying that Shield took over the thrones of many of his enemies and became their new ruler.

5. **A**

   This poem is very brief, but it provides many details about Shield. We learn that he was the son of Sheaf, an orphan, a great warrior who defeated kings and terrified other fighters, and a good king. The structure definitely provides many details about a character.

6. **B**

   Narrative poems are poems that tell a story. They include ballads, which are known for their song-like rhythm, and epic poems, which tell about the heroic efforts of a person or group of people. In this case, the poem is an example of narrative poetry not for its song-like rhythm, but rather for its focus on telling the story of a heroic warrior.

7. **B**

   This poem is an example of romanticism. Its focus on vivid descriptions of nature and strong feelings and emotions are typical of romantic poets, including Wordsworth.

8. **A**

   The last syllable of *daffodils* (*-dils*) rhymes with the word *fills*. These two words are an example of end rhyme within the poem.

9. C

The "flash" the author refers to is his memory of the daffodils. He explains that many times when he's lying on the couch alone feeling unfulfilled or thoughtful, he remembers the daffodils and instantly feels happier.

10. A

The poet is comparing the "continuous . . . stars that shine . . . on the Milky Way" to the amount of daffodils he can see lining the edge of the bay.

11. B

By depicting the dog burying the bone on the grave, the author shows the dog's indifference over the woman's death. The dog does not seem amused and is obviously not loyal because it forgot where the woman was buried. The dog also shows no remorse for digging on the grave.

12. A

The woman in the poem is speaking from her grave, so it can be assumed that when the dog says that she "passed the Gate," it is referring to the time at which she passed away.

13. D

Alliteration is the repetition of the initial sound in two or more words that appear near each other in a sentence. In this case, alliteration is demonstrated through the repetition of the *m* sound in the words *much*, *my*, and *movements*.

14. D

It is ironic that the woman describes the dog as the "one true heart" who remembers her because the dog's real reason for digging on the grave is to hide a bone, not to preserve the woman's memory.

Chapter 8
Composition

Georgia Performance Standards

ELAALRC3 **The student acquires new vocabulary in each content area and uses it correctly. The student**

   a. demonstrates an understanding of contextual vocabulary in various subjects;

   b. uses content vocabulary in writing and speaking;

   c. explores understanding of new words found in subject area texts.

ELAALRC4 **The student establishes a context for information acquired by reading across subject areas. The student**

   a. explores life experiences related to subject area content;

   b. discusses in both writing and speaking how certain words and concepts relate to multiple subjects;

   c. determines strategies for finding content and contextual meaning for unfamiliar words or concepts.

ELA11C1 **The student demonstrates understanding and control of the rules of the English language, realizing that usage involves the appropriate application of conventions and grammar in both written and spoken formats. The student**

   a. demonstrates an understanding of proper English usage and control of grammar, sentence and paragraph structure, diction, and syntax;

   b. correctly uses clauses (e.g., main and subordinate), phrases (e.g., gerund, infinitive, and participial), and mechanics of punctuation (e.g., end stops, commas, semicolons, quotations marks, colons, ellipses, hyphens);

   c. demonstrates an understanding of sentence construction (e.g., subordination, proper placement of modifiers, parallel structure) and proper English usage (e.g., consistency of verb tenses, agreement).

ELA11C2 The student demonstrates understanding of manuscript form, realizing that different forms of writing require different formats. The student

a. produces writing that conforms to appropriate manuscript requirements;

b. produces legible work that shows accurate spelling and correct use of the conventions of punctuation and capitalization;

c. reflects appropriate format requirements, including pagination, spacing, and margins, and integration of source material with appropriate citations (e.g., in-text citations, use of direct quotations, paraphrase, and summary, and weaving of source and support materials with writer's own words, etc.);

d. includes formal works cited or bibliography when applicable.

Introduction

In this chapter, you will learn how to prepare for the Georgia High School Writing Test (GHSWT). On the test, you will be asked to write a persuasive composition in response to a writing prompt. This chapter will help you to develop your composition, paying special attention to the four domains on which your composition will be scored: **ideas, organization, style,** and **conventions.** You will also be able to see a description of the scoring system for the GHSWT and have the opportunity to look at a sample composition.

GHSWT Writing Prompts

For the GHSWT, you will be asked to write a composition in response to a persuasive writing prompt. GHSWT writing prompts ask you to consider a situation, decide how you feel about the situation, and compose a persuasive piece of writing, such as one of the following:

- essay
- speech
- letter to the editor of a newspaper
- letter to your parents
- letter to your principal or school board
- editorial for the school newspaper
- paper to be presented at a city council or school board meeting

The GHSWT is administered in one two-hour session. Ninety minutes of this time is set aside to write your composition. You will also use this time to edit and revise your writing. Your composition for this test will be no more than two pages in length. The remaining time will be spent answering multiple-choice questions about revisions to essays.

Description of Persuasive Writing on the GHSWT

The GHSWT has specific criteria for what does and does not constitute an effective persuasive writing composition.

An effective persuasive composition[1]

- clearly establishes a position on the issue and fully develops an argument with specific details and examples;

- defends the writer's position with relevant evidence that is appropriate for the audience identified in the writing topic;

- demonstrates that the writer can anticipate and counter the audience's position on the issue;

- uses specific facts, personal experience and knowledge, and/or statistics to support the writer's position;

- includes appeals to logic and/or emotion;

- contains an organizational structure appropriate for persuasion;

- is multi-paragraph writing that supports a specific side of an issue;

- uses appropriate writing voice to engage the reader;

- uses precise language and varied sentences;

- introduces the reader to the issue, fully develops a position, and provides a sense of closure;

- may contain a short narrative in the introduction or a skillful extended narrative that supports the writer's position;

- contains correct sentences, usage, grammar, and spelling that make the writer's ideas understandable.

An effective persuasive composition is NOT[2]

- formulaic writing or a repetitive, standard five-paragraph formula that repeats the writer's position and supporting reasons;

- a list of irrelevant ideas or supporting details that are inappropriate for the audience identified in the writing topic;

- writing that fails to consider the reader's position on an issue;

- a list of facts, a story, and/or personal anecdotes that are unrelated to the writer's position;

[1]Retrieved from *http://gadoe.org/_documents/curriculum/testing/ga_writing_assessment_ghswt.pdf.*

[2]Retrieved from *http://gadoe.org/_documents/curriculum/testing/ga_writing_assessment_ghswt.pdf.*

- a chance for the writer to simply vent about a topic;

- writing in which ideas are presented in an illogical or confusing order;

- a single paragraph;

- flat, uninteresting writing;

- an essay that contains imprecise, ordinary language and little sentence variety;

- writing that presents ideas without introducing, developing, and/or providing closure;

- a story that does not address the persuasive purpose of the topic;

- incorrect sentences, usage, grammar, and spelling that distract the reader from the writer's ideas.

Developing Your Composition

As you begin to develop your composition, remember the three stages of writing: prewriting, drafting, and revising. You should always begin to develop your composition by prewriting. Think about the audience you will be writing for and the purpose of your writing. Once you have determined your central idea, purpose, and audience, jot down some supporting material and organize or outline your ideas into a logical sequence. Then begin the drafting stage.

In the drafting stage, you will write a rough draft of your work. An important thing to remember when writing your draft is to get your ideas down on paper. This stage of your writing does not have to be perfect. It is acceptable for the rough draft to have mistakes. These mistakes can be changed or fixed in the final stage of writing: revising.

When your rough draft is finished, begin revising and editing your work. Read your rough draft carefully. Look for mistakes in grammar, spelling, punctuation, and capitalization. Look for sentence fragments. Make sure that you have stated your main idea or that you have provided enough supporting details for readers to determine the central theme. Reword sentences or move entire paragraphs to make your writing flow in a clear, logical order. Add more details to make your writing vibrant and exciting. When you are happy with your revised draft, write the final copy of your work in the answer booklet of your test.

Content and Organization

Use strong opening and closing ideas to frame your composition. Make sure that you have addressed the reasons your topic is important and have presented a conclusion stating why you feel as you do about your topic.

Between the opening and closing of your composition are your main ideas. Make sure that your ideas are clear and that you have included a variety of main ideas and have not simply stressed the same point multiple times. Your ideas should follow a logical progression; use effective transitions so your composition flows smoothly and easily from the opening, to the main ideas, to the conclusion. Also, support your ideas with details, or reasons why you believe your ideas to be true.

Sentence Formation

Make sure that you follow traditional grammar rules when composing sentences. Check to make sure that you have placed periods and commas in logical places. Also make sure that all your sentences are not structured the same way. Variety will make your composition more interesting and more effective.

Usage

When you revise and edit, be sure to check that you have used correct verb tenses and agreements. For example, if you are writing about something that happened in the past, make certain that all the verbs you use to describe the past event are set in the past tense. Also, look at your pronouns (*I, you, he, she, it, we, they*) to make sure you have used them correctly. Examine your composition to verify that you have used words that will engage your audience. If you do not like the look or sound of a certain word in your composition, try to replace it with a better one.

Mechanics

Mechanics are the spelling, capitalization, and punctuation in your composition. If you are not sure of the spelling or capitalization of a word, look it up in a dictionary. You will not, however, be permitted to use a dictionary while taking the GHSWT.

How GHSWT Compositions Are Graded

On the GHSWT, at least two trained scorers (raters) evaluate a composition for its overall quality. Each rater assesses a composition based on the criteria of four different domains.

Description of the Analytic Scoring System for the GHSWT[3]

Domain 1: Ideas (forty percent of total score)

Components

- Controlling idea
- Supporting ideas
- Depth of development
- Sense of completeness
- Relevance of detail
- Awareness of genre

Description

- Controlling idea is focused and fully developed.
- Relevant, logical supporting ideas are appropriate to the assigned genre of writing.
- Supporting ideas are fully elaborated with appropriate examples and details.
- Response contains complete, full information.
- Response anticipates and addresses reader concerns and perspectives.

Domain 2: Organization (twenty percent of total score)

Components

- Focus
- Sequence of ideas
- Grouping of ideas within paragraphs
- Genre-specific strategies
- Transitions

Description

- Composition has a sustained focus.
- Composition includes appropriate and logical progression of ideas.
- Related ideas are grouped in a logical manner within paragraphs.
- Organizing strategy is appropriate to the assigned genre of writing and facilitates the communication of ideas.
- Varied transitional elements effectively link ideas and parts of the paper.

[3]Retrieved from *http://gadoe.org/_documents/curriculum/testing/ga_writing_assessment_ghswt.pdf.*

Domain 3: Style (twenty percent of total score)

Components

- Word choice
- Audience awareness
- Voice
- Sentence variety
- Genre-specific strategies

Description

- Writer employs appropriate, precise, and engaging language.
- Writer employs a variety of genre-specific strategies (e.g., rhetorical questions, emotional appeals) to engage the reader.
- Writer's voice is sustained throughout.
- Writer uses an effective variety of sentence beginnings, structures, and lengths.

Domain 4: Conventions (twenty percent of total score)

Components

- Sentence formation
- Usage
- Mechanics

Description

- Writer demonstrates consistently correct sentence formation in a variety of contexts: simple, complex, and compound sentences formed correctly; few sentence fragments and run-ons; functional fragments included for effect; correct end punctuation; and consistent clarity of meaning at the sentence level.
- Writer demonstrates consistently correct usage in a variety of contexts: subject-verb agreement, word forms (nouns, adjectives, adverbs), pronoun-antecedent agreement, verb tense, and commonly confused homonyms.
- Writer demonstrates consistently correct mechanics in a variety of contexts: punctuation within sentences, spelling, capitalization, and paragraph indentation.

After assessing the composition based on the above criteria, each rater assigns a composition a score from 1 to 4 in each of the four domains. The raters' scores in the ideas domain are doubled so that this domain represents forty percent of a student's score. All scores are then added and combined to arrive at a total score for each student. These scores are then converted to a scale score ranging from 400 to 600 points. A score of at least 500 is required to pass the GHSWT.

Student Writing Checklist for Persuasive Writing

The Student Writing Checklist for Persuasive Writing will appear on the GHSWT. It is designed to guide you in creating a top-scoring composition.

Student Writing Checklist for Persuasive Writing[5]

Prepare yourself to write:

- [ ] Read the *Writing Situation* and *Directions for Writing* carefully.
- [ ] Brainstorm for ideas.
- [ ] Consider how to address your audience.
- [ ] Decide what ideas to include and how to organize them.
- [ ] Write only in English.

Make your paper meaningful:

- [ ] Use your knowledge and/or personal experiences that are related to the topic.
- [ ] Express a clear point of view.
- [ ] Fully support your argument with specific details, examples, and convincing reasons.
- [ ] Include an appeal to logic and/or emotions.
- [ ] Present your ideas in a clear and logical order.
- [ ] Stay on topic.

Make your paper interesting to read:

- [ ] Use examples and details that would be convincing to your audience.
- [ ] Use appropriate voice that shows your interest in the topic.
- [ ] Use precise, descriptive, vivid words.
- [ ] Vary the type, structure, and length of your sentences.
- [ ] Use effective transitions.

Edit and revise your paper:

- [ ] Consider rearranging your ideas and changing words to make your paper more effective.
- [ ] Add additional information or details to make your paper complete.
- [ ] Proofread your paper for usage, punctuation, capitalization, and spelling.

[5]Retrieved from *http://gadoe.org/_documents/curriculum/testing/ga_writing_assessment_ghswt.pdf.*

Sample GHSWT Writing Prompt

Now read this sample writing prompt. An example of a top-scoring composition follows the prompt.

Writing Situation

At a recent school board meeting, your principal was informed that your high school's expenses are exceeding the school's budget for the year. In an effort to cut back on expenses, your principal has asked the school board for permission to cancel all field trips for the remainder of the year, citing field trips as "vacations" from learning, and therefore, an unnecessary expense. Decide whether you agree or disagree with your principal.

Directions for Writing

Write a letter to the school board that clearly states your position on the necessity of field trips for the rest of the year. Try to convince the board members to agree with your position using well-developed arguments.

Sample Top-Scoring Composition

The following is a sample response to the prompt you have just read. Notice that the sample clearly responds to the prompt. It contains a good opening and closing and progresses logically from beginning to end. The composition is well developed and stays focused on the topic throughout. It contains few, if any, errors on usage, sentence construction, and mechanics. It sounds authentic and original and expresses the writer's individual or unique perspective.

Dear School Board,

I am aware that you were recently contacted by Mr. Henry, principal of Westmore High School, regarding permission to cancel the school's field trips for the rest of the year. While I understand the need to conserve school money to stay within the fixed budget, I am convinced that we can find alternate sources of funding without having to cancel our field trips.

Some people, such as Mr. Henry, think that field trips are vacations from learning. I understand how some people might make this mistake. Students get to take a break from the monotony of a school day, get on a bus, and travel to a theater, an art museum, a science center, or a historical site. They get to watch plays, see magnificent works of art, try new inventions, or experience life as it was in the past. These are all fun activities that some might view as purely recreational.

What people seem to forget, however, is that these field trips do not allow us to take a vacation from our education. Rather, field trips allow us to enhance what we've learned in the classroom. Although books, chalkboards, and lectures are important, hands-on learning gives students the opportunity to take what they have learned and see how it is applied in real life. Why silently read a play when you can see it performed live? Why study paintings in a book when you can look at them in person? Why study pictures of the parts of a flower when you can visit a greenhouse and study the real thing? Field trips provide us not only with a break from the monotony of a regular school day, but also with a chance to supplement what we learn in the classroom with hands-on experiences.

For these reasons, it is my belief that funding for field trips should not be cut. Instead, maybe we could enhance our budget in other ways, such as bake sales or parental donations. If those of us within this educational community put our heads together, I'm sure we can come up with a better solution for our students. I thank you for taking the time to consider my thoughts on this issue.

Sincerely,

Patrick Grier

Revising Your Writing

When you write your persuasive essay for the GHSWT, you may have to revise your draft before you are satisfied with your composition. However, you will also have to practice revising on the Georgia High School Graduation Test (GHSGT).

On the GHSGT, you will be asked to answer multiple-choice (MC) questions on revision. You may be asked to choose the sentence that is written correctly, meaning the sentence with correct grammar and punctuation. You may be asked to read a passage and then choose the necessary revision to make the passage correct. You might also have to choose a sentence that would be best to include in a certain type of writing.

Revision Practice for the GHSGT

The following are examples of revision questions that will be asked on the GHSGT.

    Read each question. Then use the Tip underneath each question to help you choose the correct answer. When you finish, read the answer explanations at the end of this chapter.

 Questions

Read the following passage and answer question 1.

Gabe didn't get no books at the library; he looked in the card catalog, scanned the shelves, and went home.

1. What revision, if any, is needed in the passage?

   A. Change *catalog* to *cataloge*.

   B. Change the semicolon after *library* to a comma.

   C. Change *no* to *any*.

   D. No revision is needed.

 | Look at the passage and determine if it contains an error in spelling, grammar, or punctuation. If you cannot spot an error, try making the changes in each of the answer choices to see if any will make the passage correct.

2. Which of the sentences below is written correctly?

   A. We went to the store, and Jan buys a bag of oranges.

   B. We go to the store, and Jan will buy a bag of oranges.

   C. We went to the store, and Jan bought a bag of oranges.

   D. We go the store, and Jan will have bought a bag of oranges.

 | This question deals with verb tense. Some of the choices may contain improper shifts in verb tense. Read the answer choices. In which choice is verb tense used correctly?

Read the following passage and answer question 3.

Sandra's speech on global politics was very moving. Her teacher was also very impressed with her research.

3. What revision, if any, is needed in the passage?

    A. Change *was* to *is*.

    B. Change the period after *moving* to a colon.

    C. Change *politics* to *political*.

    D. No revision is needed.

 TIP Does this sentence contain any errors in spelling, punctuation, or grammar? Try to make some of the changes suggested in the answer choices. Do any of these change make the passage correct?

4. Which of the sentences below is written correctly?

    A. Jackie is the most disorganized person in the class.

    B. Jackie is the person with the most disorganized in the class.

    C. Jackie is the more disorganized person in the class.

    D. Jackie is the person who is like the most disorganized in the class.

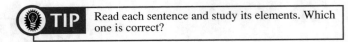 **TIP** Read each sentence and study its elements. Which one is correct?

Read the following passage and answer question 5.

Tom has the horrible sense of direction; he got lost on his way home.

5. What revision, if any, is needed in the passage?

    A. Change *sense* to *since*.

    B. Change *the* to *a*.

    C. Change the period after *direction* to a question mark.

    D. No revision is needed.

 TIP Try altering the sentence according to each of the suggested changes in the answer choices. Would any of these revisions make the sentence correct in grammar, punctuation, and spelling?

6. Which sentence below is written correctly?

   A. This one is that women's umbrella, and this one is yours'.

   B. This one is that womans' umbrella, and this one is yours.

   C. This one is that woman's umbrella, and this one is yours.

   D. This one is that woman's umbrella, and this one is yours'.

 Try to remember the correct ways to use an apostrophe to show possession. Which sentence correctly expresses possession?

7. Suppose you are writing an essay about preventing pollution in the world's oceans. Which is the **best** way to state your research question?

   A. Why is medical waste found in the ocean?

   B. What are the major sources of ocean pollution?

   C. How can we stop people from polluting the Atlantic Ocean?

   D. When can we make our environment cleaner?

 Reread the question and consider the specific topic of your essay. Which of these questions would best help you find relevant information for an essay on this topic?

8. Which sentence would be **best** to include in a letter to the school board about getting new equipment in the school gym?

   A. The basketballs don't even bounce—what good is that?

   B. We didn't ruin the equipment, so you shouldn't punish us for it.

   C. Some of the equipment is old and unsafe for students to use.

   D. I know that all of this sports stuff really isn't that expensive.

 Think about the audience of this letter. Which sentence would be most effective in getting across the point that new equipment is needed? Which would most likely convince a school board member that new equipment is necessary?

9. Suppose you were writing a report about America's need to adopt renewable energy sources. Which would be the **best** way to state your research question?

   A. How is solar energy harnessed and turned into usable energy?

   B. Which has been the most successful renewable energy source?

   C. When will the world come to depend on renewable energy?

   D. What renewable energy options are available in this country?

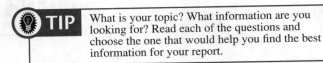

TIP What is your topic? What information are you looking for? Read each of the questions and choose the one that would help you find the best information for your report.

10. Which sentence would be **best** to include in a speech to local government officials arguing that cosmetic companies should be prohibited from animal testing?

   A. Animals don't even use cosmetics, so this is not fair.

   B. It is unethical to torture animals for the vanity of humans.

   C. Rabbits are so cute and they should never be hurt.

   D. Cosmetics aren't good for your skin anyway, so stop using them.

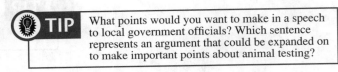

TIP What points would you want to make in a speech to local government officials? Which sentence represents an argument that could be expanded on to make important points about animal testing?

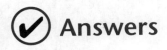

Answers

1. C

   As it is, the sentence contains a double negative—*didn't* and *no*—which is an error in grammar. Changing the *no* to *any* removes the double negative.

2. C

   Answer choice C contains two past-tense verbs. Other choices contained mixed verb tenses that were used incorrectly.

3. D

   No revision is needed. This passage is grammatically correct and contains no errors.

4. A

   The sentence in answer choice A is grammatically correct. Answer choice B and D don't make sense. Answer choice C would be okay except the word "more" is used to compare two people or things. Jackie isn't being compared to anyone. Answer choice A is best.

5. B

   The grammatical revision in answer choice B makes the sentence correct.

6. C

   This sentence correctly uses apostrophes to show possession of the two umbrellas. The word "woman" is singular; it refers to one woman. The word "women" is plural; it refers to more than one woman. This sentence refers to one woman and one umbrella, so answer choice C is the correct answer.

7. B

   This question relates directly to the topic of preventing pollution in the world's oceans. Answer choice A mentions a specific type of pollution, and choice C mentions a specific ocean, neither of which relate to the broader topic of pollution in the world's oceans. Choice D mentions the environment in general, which is far too broad a topic.

8. C

   Stressing to the school board that the current equipment is dangerous for students is the best way to convince the school board that new equipment in needed. The other choices are either too vague or do not relate directly to the topic and use language that is inappropriate for the audience of the letter.

9. D

   Answer choice D focuses directly on the use of renewable energy in America. The other choices focus on specific types of renewable energy and the global use of renewable energy, which only indirectly relate to the topic.

10. B

   Answer choice B is the only point that is not off topic. The other choices indirectly relate to the topic, but would not be effective for the purpose of the speech.

Georgia High School Graduation Test

ELA Practice Test 1

Read the passage and answer the question that follows.

Majestic Redwoods

It is difficult to describe a redwood tree. These trees are so large and beautiful that they take your breath away. A redwood tree grows from a seed no bigger than a seed from any other plant. However, when it is fully grown, a redwood tree might be as tall as a skyscraper!

Some redwood trees are very old. For example, a few have been around since the days of the dinosaurs! If nothing destroys a redwood tree, it will live many, many years.

Many redwood trees grow along California's north coast. The climate there is perfect for redwoods. The air is cool and moist. Redwoods grow well in this environment.

PT1 Which assertion is **best** supported by the evidence in the above passage?

A. Redwood trees cannot survive outside California.
B. Pollen from redwood trees can affect breathing.
C. People are the greatest threat to redwood trees.
D. Redwood trees are almost too beautiful for words.

Read the following passage and answer question 1.

Yolanda waited anxiously for the captain of the cheerleading squad to post the results. She felt that the audition had gone good. However, she was still worried. She thought that her final handspring could have been better.

1. What revision, if any, is needed in the passage?

    A. Change *better* to *best*.
    B. Change the comma after *However* to a semicolon.
    C. Change *good* to *well*.
    D. No correction is needed.

2. Suppose you are writing an essay about the nutritional quality of the lunches served at your school. Which of the following is the **best** way to state your research question?

    A. What is our local school board doing to make our school's lunches healthier to eat?
    B. Do our school's lunches meet the nutritional standards set up by the state government?
    C. What differences exist between our school lunches and the lunches at other schools?
    D. What is the relationship between the nutritional value of school lunches and higher test scores?

Passage 1

Read the following speech and answer questions 3 through 8.

Is It a Crime for a Citizen of the United States to Vote?

by Susan B. Anthony

Before the nineteenth amendment was passed in 1920, Susan B. Anthony shocked people by daring to vote in the 1872 presidential election. Several days later, she was arrested and charged with "illegal voting." Anthony pleaded "not guilty" to these charges and then traveled around the country, campaigning for women's right to vote.

Friends and Fellow-citizens: I stand before you to-night, under indictment for the alleged crime of having voted at the last Presidential election, without having a lawful right to vote. It shall be my work this evening to prove to you that in thus voting, I not only committed no crime, but, instead, simply exercised my citizen's right, guaranteed to me and all United States citizens by the National Constitution, beyond the power of any State to deny.

Our democratic-republican government is based on the idea of the natural right of every individual member thereof to a voice and a vote in making and executing the laws. We assert the province of government to be to secure the people in the enjoyment of their unalienable rights. We throw to the winds the old dogma that governments can give rights. Before governments were organized, no one denies that each individual possessed the right to protect his own life, liberty and property. And when 100 or 1,000,000 people enter into a free government, they do not barter away their natural rights; they simply pledge themselves to protect each other in the enjoyment of them, through prescribed judicial and legislative tribunals. They agree to abandon the methods of brute force in the adjustment of their differences, and adopt those of civilization.

Nor can you find a word in any of the grand documents left us by the fathers that assumes for government the power to create or to confer rights. The Declaration of Independence, the United States Constitution, the constitutions of the several states and the <u>organic</u> laws of the territories, all alike propose to protect the people in the exercise of their . . . rights. Not one of them pretends to bestow rights.

> "All men are created equal . . . with certain unalienable rights. Among these are life, liberty and the pursuit of happiness. That to secure these, governments are instituted among men, deriving their just powers from the consent of the governed."

Here is no shadow of government authority over rights, nor exclusion of any from their full and equal enjoyment. . . . And here, in this very first paragraph of the declaration, is the assertion of the natural right of all to the ballot; for, how can "the consent of the governed" be given, if the right to vote be denied. Again:

> "That whenever any form of government becomes destructive of these ends, it is the right of the people to alter or abolish it, and to institute a new government, laying its foundations on such principles, and organizing its powers in such forms as to them shall seem most likely to effect their safety and happiness."

Surely, the right of the whole people to vote is here clearly implied. For however destructive in their happiness this government might become, a disfranchised class could neither alter nor abolish it, nor institute a new one, except by the old brute force method of insurrection and rebellion. One-half of the people of this nation to-day are utterly powerless to blot from the statute books an unjust law, or to write there a new and a just one. The women, dissatisfied as they are with this form of government, that enforces taxation without representation, —that compels them to obey laws to which they have never given their consent, —that imprisons and hangs them without a trial by a jury of their peers, that robs them, in marriage, of the custody of their own persons, wages and children, —are this half of the people left wholly at the mercy of the other half, in direct violation of the spirit and letter of the declarations of the framers of this government, every one of which was based on the immutable principle of equal rights to all. . .

The preamble of the federal constitution says:

> "We, the people of the United States, in order to form a more perfect union, establish justice, insure domestic tranquility, provide for the common defense, promote the general welfare and secure the blessings of liberty to ourselves and our posterity, do ordain and established this constitution for the United States of America."

> It was we, the people, not we, the white male citizens, nor yet we, the male citizens; but we, the whole people, who formed this Union. And we formed it, not to give the blessings or liberty, but to secure them; not to the half of ourselves and the half of our posterity, but to the whole people—women as well as men. And it is downright mockery to talk to women of their enjoyment of the blessings of liberty while they are denied the use of the only means of securing them provided by this democratic-republican government—the ballot.

Go On

3. For which audience does Ms. Anthony address the above speech?

   A. all of the citizens of her hometown
   B. the female citizens of the United States
   C. members of the federal government
   D. all of the citizens of the United States

4. Which **best** describes how this speech is structured?

   A. an opinion followed by supporting details
   B. a list of the speaker's best characteristics
   C. a problem followed by several solutions
   D. a sequence of historical events

5. Throughout the speech, the speaker uses examples to

   A. convince people that she is right.
   B. compare two different ideas.
   C. help support her own opinion.
   D. explain an opposing viewpoint.

6. What is the **most likely** reason Ms. Anthony gave this speech?

   A. She wanted to prove that she didn't commit a crime when she voted.
   B. She wanted to show that women have as much right to vote as men.
   C. She wanted to convince other women to send letters of protest.
   D. She wanted to demand an apology for the way was treated.

7. As used in the passage, <u>organic</u> **most** nearly means

   A. *just.*
   B. *great.*
   C. *basic.*
   D. *former.*

8. The point of view used in the passage reveals the speaker's

   A. distrust of government.
   B. feelings of superiority.
   C. frustration with unjust laws.
   D. desire to prove her innocence.

Go On

Passage 2

Read the following passage and answer questions 9 through 15.

Excerpt from *The Odyssey*

by Homer

Translated by Samuel Butler

The Greek epic The Odyssey tells the story of Odysseus, the king of Ithaca, and the events of his ten-year journey home after the Trojan War. After suffering many hardships, Odysseus and his men land on the Aegean Island, home of the goddess and sorceress Circe.

When they reached Circe's[1] house they found it built of cut stones, on a site that could be seen from far, in the middle of the forest. There were wild mountain wolves and lions prowling all round it—poor bewitched creatures whom she had tamed by her enchantments and drugged into subjection. They did not attack my men, but wagged their great tails, fawned upon them, and rubbed their noses lovingly against them. As hounds crowd round their master when they see him coming from dinner—for they know he will bring them something—even so did these wolves and lions with their great claws fawn upon my men, but the men were terribly frightened at seeing such strange creatures.

"Presently they reached the gates of the goddess's house, and as they stood there they could hear Circe within, singing most beautifully as she worked at her loom, making a web so fine, so soft, and of such dazzling colours as no one but a goddess could weave. On this Polites, whom I valued and trusted more than any other of my men, said, 'There is some one inside working at a loom and singing most beautifully; the whole place resounds with it, let us call her and see whether she is woman or goddess.'

"They called her and she came down, unfastened the door, and bade them enter. They, thinking no evil, followed her, all except Eurylochus, who suspected mischief and staid outside. When she had got them into her house, she set them upon benches and seats and mixed them a mess with cheese, honey, meal, and Pramnian wine, but she drugged it with wicked poisons to make them forget their homes, and when they had drunk she turned them into pigs by a stroke of her wand, and shut them up in her pigstyes. They were like pigs—head, hair, and all, and they grunted just as pigs do; but their senses were the same as before, and they remembered everything.

"Thus then were they shut up squealing, and Circe threw them some acorns and beech masts such as pigs eat, but Eurylochus hurried back to tell me about the sad fate of our comrades. He was so overcome with dismay that though he tried to speak he could find no words to do so; his eyes filled with tears and he could only sob and sigh, till at last we forced his story out of him, and he told us what had happened to the others. . . .

"With this I left the ship and went up inland. When I got through the charmed grove, and was near the great house of the enchantress Circe, I met Mercury[2] with his golden wand, disguised as a young man in the hey-day of his youth and beauty with the down just coming upon his face. He came up to me and took my hand within his own, saying, 'My poor unhappy man, whither are you going over this mountain top, alone and without knowing the way? Your men are shut up in Circe's pigstyes, like so many wild boars in their lairs. You surely do not fancy that you can set them free? I can tell you that you will never get back and will have to stay there with the rest of them. But never mind, I will protect you and get you out of your difficulty. Take this herb, which is one of great virtue, and keep it about you when you go to Circe's house, it will be a <u>talisman</u> to you against every kind of mischief. . . .'

"When I got to the gates I stood there and called the goddess, and as soon as she heard me she came down, opened the door, and asked me to come in; so I followed her—much troubled in my mind. She set me on a richly decorated seat inlaid with silver, there was a footstool also under my feet, and she mixed a mess in a golden goblet for me to drink; but she drugged it, for she meant me mischief. When she had given it me, and I had drunk it without its charming me, she struck me with her wand. 'There now,' she cried, 'be off to the pigstye, and make your lair with the rest of them.'

"But I rushed at her with my sword drawn as though I would kill her, whereon she fell with a loud scream, clasped my knees, and spoke piteously, saying, 'Who and whence are you? From what place and people have you come? How can it be that my drugs have no power to charm you? Never yet was any man able to stand so much as a taste of the herb I gave you; you must be spell-proof; surely you can be none other than the bold hero Ulysses[3], who Mercury always said would come here some day with his ship while on his way home from Troy; so be it then; sheathe your sword and let us . . . make friends and learn to trust each other.'

"And I answered, 'Circe, how can you expect me to be friendly with you when you have just been turning all my men into pigs? . . . You must free my men and bring them to me that I may see them with my own eyes.'

"When I had said this she went straight through the court with her wand in her hand and opened the pigstye doors. My men came out like so many prime hogs and stood looking at her, but she went about among them and anointed each with a second drug, whereon the bristles that the bad drug had given them fell off, and they became men again, younger than they were before, and much taller and better looking. They knew me at once, seized me each of them by the hand, and wept for joy till the whole house was filled with the sound of their halloa-ballooing, and Circe herself was so sorry for them that she came up to me and said, 'Ulysses, noble son of Laertes, go back at once to the sea where you have left your ship, and first draw it on to the land. Then, hide all your ship's gear and property in some cave, and come back here with your men. . . . I know how much you have all of you suffered at sea, and how ill you have fared among cruel savages on the mainland, but that is over now, so stay here, and eat and drink till you are once more as strong and hearty as you were when you left Ithaca; for at present you are weakened both in body and mind; you keep all the time thinking of the hardships you have suffered during your travels, so that you have no more cheerfulness left in you.'

Go On

"We stayed with Circe for a whole twelvemonth feasting upon an untold quantity both of meat and wine. But when the year had passed in the waning of moons and the long days had come round, my men called me apart and said, 'Sir, it is time you began to think about going home, if so be you are to be spared to see your house and native country at all. . . .'

"The goddess listened to what I had got to say. 'Circe,' said I, 'please to keep the promise you made me about furthering me on my homeward voyage. I want to get back and so do my men. . . .'

"And the goddess answered, 'Ulysses, noble son of Laertes, you shall none of you stay here any longer if you do not want to, but there is another journey which you have got to take before you can sail homewards. You must go to the house of Hades[4]. . .' "

---

[1]Circe: sorceress and enchantress; daughter of Helios, the sun god
[2]Mercury: messenger to the gods; patron of travelers, merchants, rogues, and thieves
[3]Ulysses: Latin name for Odysseus
[4]Hades: the underworld; world of the dead

9. As used in the passage, talisman **most** nearly means

    A. *guide.*
    B. *charm.*
    C. *cure.*
    D. *symbol.*

10. Circe **most likely** turned the men into pigs

    A. to hurt Ulysses.
    B. to anger Mercury.
    C. so they looked funny.
    D. so they had to stay with her.

11. Which **best** describes the way in which the passage is structured?

    A. a problem followed by a solution
    B. main idea with supporting details
    C. details describing a character
    D. a sequence of events

Go On

12. The point of view in the passage reveals

    A. Ulysses' loyalty to his men.
    B. Mercury's anger toward Circe.
    C. Circe's faith in Ulysses.
    D. Ulysses' love for Circe.

13. The author depicts Circe's singing as sounding beautiful to the men's ears to show Circe's

    A. generous hospitality.
    B. sweet nature.
    C. enchanting powers.
    D. musical talent.

14. Which word **best** describes Mercury's tone in paragraph 5?

    A. hostile
    B. defensive
    C. astonished
    D. sympathetic

15. Which assertion is **best** supported by the evidence in the passage?

    A. Circe has as much power as the gods and goddesses.
    B. Ulysses cannot be tricked as easily as his men.
    C. A true hero will always remain loyal to his friends.
    D. Gods and goddesses were unconcerned with humans.

Go On

Read the following passage and answer question 16.

After Ryan stayed out passed curfew and flunked an English exam, his parents decided that he should stay in one weekend and study. Ryan was outraged. He had already made plans to see a movie with friends that Saturday night!

16. What revision, if any, is needed in the passage?

   A. Change *passed* to *past*.
   B. Change *outraged* to *outrageous*.
   C. Change the comma after *exam* to a semicolon.
   D. No correction is needed.

17. Which of the following sentences is written correctly?

   A. You better be home before nine: otherwise, you will be grounded.
   B. You better be home before nine; otherwise, you will be grounded.
   C. You better be home before nine, otherwise you will be grounded.
   D. You better be home before nine, otherwise, you will be grounded.

Stop

Passage 3

Read the following poem and answer questions 18 through 23.

The Spring and the Fall

by Edna St. Vincent Millay

Twentieth-century poet Edna St. Vincent Millay was born in Maine in 1892. She was one of the most famous poets of her time.

> In the spring of the year, in the spring of the year,
> I walked the road beside my dear.
> The trees were black where the bark was wet.
> I see them yet, in the spring of the year.
> 5 He broke me a bough of the blossoming peach
> That was out of the way and hard to reach.
>
> In the fall of the year, in the fall of the year,
> I walked the road beside my dear.
> The rooks went up with a raucous trill.
> 10 I hear them still, in the fall of the year.
> He laughed at all I dared to praise,
> And broke my heart, in little ways.
>
> Year be springing or year be falling,
> The bark will drip and the birds be calling.
> 15 There's much that's fine to see and hear
> In the spring of a year, in the fall of a year.
> 'Tis not love's going hurt my days.
> But that it went in little ways.

---

18. The point of view in the poem reveals the poet's

A. longing for the man that left her behind.
B. hope that her lover will return someday.
C. desire to escape her memories of the past.
D. disappointment in how her relationship ended.

19. Throughout the poem, the images of "spring" and "fall" are symbols for

    A. morning and evening.
    B. beginning and end.
    C. love and hatred.
    D. birth and death.

20. Which pair of words from the poem is an example of end rhyme?

    A. *wet* and *yet*
    B. *year* and *dear*
    C. *rooks* and *road*
    D. *broke* and *bough*

21. This poem is an example of lyric poetry because of its

    A. use of blank verse.
    B. use of slant rhyme.
    C. focus on telling a story.
    D. focus on inner feelings.

22. As used in the poem, the phrase "And broke my heart, in little ways" is an example of which literary device?

    A. assonance
    B. alliteration
    C. idiom
    D. tone

23. Which **best** describes the way in which the poem is structured?

    A. comparison and contrast
    B. a main idea with anecdotes
    C. details describing a character
    D. a question followed by an answer

Passage 4

Read the following passage and answer questions 24 through 30.

Attention: Management Office

Merrymakers Movie Theater
90210 Silver Screen Street
Savannah, GA 31322

To Whom It May Concern:

I have been a loyal customer of Merrymakers Movie Theater for years. I have never damaged any company property, been disruptive while in your facility, or disrespected any company employees. Despite this spotless record, my friends and I were escorted out of a Savannah theater's lobby by security last Friday evening before we even had a chance to see the movie for which we had purchased tickets.

Allow me to recount the events of that evening. Last Friday was my sixteenth birthday. My friends and I planned on enjoying dinner and a movie to <u>commemorate</u> the event. Our parents dropped us off at the diner across the street from the theater for dinner and agreed to pick us up after the movie was over. None of our parents had any interest in seeing the big movie opening that weekend, *Assignment: Unachievable 7*. We had done this dozens of times before and had never experienced any problems.

After dinner, the seven of us walked across the street to the theater. We went into the lobby to the ticket kiosk. Since my mom had purchased our tickets for us online earlier in the day, all we had to do was enter the confirmation number and wait for our tickets to print. Once we were finished, a few of my friends went to purchase refreshments while my friend Jackie and I went to find some seats. When we handed our tickets to the usher, he asked us where our parents were. We told him that our parents were not attending the movie with us. The usher called for security on his walkie-talkie and asked us to step out of line. We asked the usher to explain the problem, but he refused to answer us.

The security guard took us back to the main lobby. Our other friends, with bags of popcorn and soda bottles in their hands, saw what was happening and met us in the lobby. The security guard explained that the movie theater had recently adopted new rules concerning unaccompanied minors. These rules state that anyone under the age of eighteen is not permitted inside the theater after 9:30 p.m. without adult supervision. Though the movie was rated PG-13 and we had already purchased our tickets, we were told that we would not be able to attend the show because its start time was scheduled for 9:25 p.m., five minutes before the curfew begins. We were given a refund of my mother's money and my friends and I allowed the security guard to escort us from the theater without incident. Our parents promptly picked us up fifteen minutes later.

One might think that I am merely writing to complain that this new policy ruined what should have been a wonderful evening or express how much I dislike the company now. This is not the case. I still feel that Merrymakers Movie Theater is the "best seat in the city." However, I hope

Go On

that company officials will remember that teenagers continue to be one of the largest groups of consumers in the United States today. By enforcing this new curfew, the company will not only lose money on ticket sales, but also make some of its biggest customers feel like "second-class" citizens.

It is understandable for a company to worry about security. It is also true that some juveniles can be rowdy and cause problems. However, the actions of one or two individuals should not be the standard by which a company judges all minors. It is unfair to label us as uncontrollable hoodlums bent on causing a stir whenever possible. Some of us are loyal customers who just want to enjoy a movie with our friends. We really aren't all that different from adults in this respect.

I urge the company to consider revising the current policy. If the company fails to do this, my friends and I will be left with no choice but to find another theater that doesn't treat us like children and respects our rights as consumers.

Sincerely,

Amber Madison

24. The point of view in the passage reveals the writer's

    A. anger at having her birthday ruined.
    B. disappointment over missing the movie.
    C. feelings that she has been treated unfairly.
    D. hope that Merrymakers will enforce stricter policies.

25. As used in the passage, <u>commemorate</u> **most** nearly means

    A. *study*.
    B. *witness*.
    C. *celebrate*.
    D. *announce*.

26. The writer explains her history with Merrymakers Movie Theater in order to

    A. express the outrage she feels.
    B. show that she is a good student.
    C. demand that they refund her mother's money.
    D. explain that she has been a loyal customer.

Go On

27. For which audience does the writer address the passage?

     A. Merrymakers Movie Theater ushers
     B. Merrymakers Movie Theater security
     C. Merrymakers Movie Theater managers
     D. Merrymakers Move Theater customers

28. Which **best** describes how this passage is structured?

     A. a sequence of events is presented
     B. a problem followed by several solutions
     C. an opinion followed by supporting details
     D. a list of the writer's best characteristics

29. Which word **best** describes the writer's tone in the final paragraph?

     A. hostile
     B. reluctant
     C. sarcastic
     D. sympathetic

30. Which assertion is **best** supported by the evidence in the passage?

     A. Merrymakers Movie Theater doesn't like teenagers.
     B. Parents need to better supervise their teenagers.
     C. Some teenagers feel that broad restrictions are unfair.
     D. Teenagers cause the most problems at movie theaters.

31. Which of the following sentences is written correctly?

     A. Tim is buying balloons and buying streamers and buying confetti for the party.
     B. Tim is buying balloons and streamers and confetti for the party.
     C. Tim is buying balloons, streamers, and confetti for the party.
     D. Tim is buying balloons streamers and confetti for the party.

Go On

Read the following passage and answer question 32.

Paula wants to go to the mall; however, she still has chores to finish. She must clean her room, do her laundry, and walk the dog before she will be permitted to go.

32. Which revision, if any, is needed in the passage?

    A. Change the semicolon after *mall* to a colon.
    B. Remove the comma after *laundry*.
    C. Change *permitted* to *permission*.
    D. No correction is needed.

Go On

Passage 5

Read the following passage and answer questions 33 through 38.

All about the Music

Sela, a member of a band about to perform at a club, is trying to figure out how to deal with her stage fright.

While they waited impatiently to go on stage, Shaz and Zoë rehearsed their tra-la-las in the hallway, preparing their voices for the concert. As usual, Sela was panicking: pacing, sweating, sucking on mentholated cough drops to soothe her throat, and reciting the lyrics repeatedly.

Lost in anxiety, Sela bumped into Jorge, who, not noticing Sela's oblivious stare, asked if she was excited for the band's performance. His dad worked at the Roxy Club and had arranged for Sela's band to play that night. Sela had pleaded him for the opportunity, but now that it was happening, she was beyond petrified.

When Jorge asked Sela what was bothering her, Sela explained that she always got nervous before a gig. Since this was the band's biggest crowd yet, she was the most fearful she had ever been. She could practice for a thousand hours, but when the moment of reckoning arrived, she felt like she needed to lose her lunch.

Jorge assured her that he knew lots of tricks to conquer stage fright. "Pick a friendly, smiling face in the audience," he explained, "and keep your eyes on that smile the whole time; play just to that person if you have to."

Sela thanked him, but she felt that her <u>trepidation</u> was much greater than what tricks could fix. Despite playing piano for most of her life, she was beginning to worry that maybe she wasn't destined for performing. In her room, she could take out the keyboard and play perfectly for hours. She could hum a new tune, and her hands would gambol across the keys instinctively, the melody teeming, but if her little brother entered the room, her gift vanished like a ghost.

Sela listened to Shaz and Zoë, who were harmonizing brilliantly in the wings. Sela asked them how they stayed so composed.

Shaz explained that she ignored the audience completely: "I pretend there's a big wall between us so I can't get to them, and more importantly, they can't get to me." She gave a look that a lion might give a rabbit, a get-out-of-my-way-before-I-bite-you kind of gaze. Her rationale seemed sensible, but Sela was positive it wouldn't work for her. She already thought of the audience as her adversary, and that wasn't working.

Go On

"What's the point of performing if there isn't an audience?" Zoë asked. Even Zoë's speaking voice made people swoon because it was distinctive and melodic. Zoë looked fantastic and sounded better, and it was no mystery to Sela that Zoë wasn't the least bit troubled by performing.

Zoë's fearlessness terrified Sela; she started to think that perhaps she wasn't meant to be an entertainer. She thought that maybe she was meant to be a music writer who sat at home and played her piano and didn't bother with performing. For her entire life, Sela had fantasized about mounting a stage and rocking an audience, but when it mattered most, she lost her nerve.

Sela knew the minutes before show time were disappearing, and she began to tremble. She paced past the fog machine, the manufactured smoke chilly on her damp skin, and Jules walked out from behind a gigantic amplifier. With her drumsticks, she was counting out a beat on the palm of her hand, and she took a break to wipe sweat from her forehead.

Sela was about to say that Jules had nothing to be worried about because all Jules had to do was pound out a beat. She could disappear into the back of the stage and hide behind her huge drum kit. She didn't have to stare at those keys swimming together, becoming indistinguishable. Just as Sela was about to go into this diatribe, Jules spoke.

"I wish I were more like you," Jules said. "You know, a born performer."

Sela looked at Jules peculiarly. What was she talking about?

"I mean, sometimes I look at you up there, right at the edge of the stage, playing and singing so magnificently, and I don't know how you do it."

Sela contemplated this because she had never imagined that someone felt this way about her. She was constantly in awe of people she thought were good performers, and it was hard to acknowledge that someone perceived her that way.

"You know how I deal with my stage fright?" Jules asked in a low and timid voice, and Sela waited for her to continue.

"I pretend that I'm you, that I'm confident and self-assured and above all, that I'm really, really talented."

The announcer introduced Sela's band and Jules walked past Sela and into the spotlight. Along with the rest of the girls, Sela stepped out in front of the audience, into the applause and the excitement and this new feeling, not like apprehension at all. Instead, Sela felt like the crowd and the song and the band were all one. The audience wasn't a distraction anymore; the crowd was like a chorus or a bridge, just one more part of the music.

---

33. As used in the passage, <u>trepidation</u> **most** nearly means

    A. *shyness.*
    B. *excitement.*
    C. *anxiety.*
    D. *astonishment.*

Go On

34. Which statement from the passage **best** reflects the climax?

   A. Zoë's fearlessness terrified Sela; she started to think that perhaps she wasn't meant to be an entertainer.
   B. Sela contemplated this because she had never imagined that someone felt this way about her.
   C. Sela had pleaded him for the opportunity, but now that it was happening, she was beyond petrified.
   D. Zoë looked fantastic and sounded better, and it was no mystery to Sela that Zoë wasn't the least bit troubled by performing.

35. The author depicts Shaz trying to teach Sela the look that she gives to the audience in order to show Shaz's

   A. insecurity.
   B. optimism.
   C. enthusiasm.
   D. fearlessness.

36. Which **best** describes the way in which the passage is structured?

   A. a sequence of events
   B. a conflict followed by the resolution
   C. comparison and contrast
   D. cause and effect

37. As used to describe Sela's musical talents, the phrase "vanished like a ghost" is an example of which literary device?

   A. metaphor
   B. personification
   C. hyperbole
   D. simile

38. Which of the following events in the passage is an example of irony?

   A. Shaz and Zoë rehearsing their songs in the hallway
   B. Jules pretending to be Sela to overcome her stage fright
   C. Jorge advising Sela to pick out a friendly face in the audience
   D. Zoë explaining that the point of performing is to please the audience

Go On

Passage 6

Read the following passage and answer questions 39 through 45.

Savannah Fire

Sixteen-year-old Charlotte Mitchell is poking around in her attic when she makes an interesting discovery.

Hazy, grayish-yellow sunlight filtered through the tiny attic window and illuminated the dust particles floating in the air. Charlotte Mitchell ascended the last creaky step and peered around her at the remnants of generations past. She knew that her house, which stood prominently at the edge of the city of Savannah, had been in her family for nearly two hundred years. What she hadn't realized was that during those two hundred years, no one had ever attempted to clean the attic.

Charlotte picked her way toward a rocking chair blanketed by a dusty white sheet. Settling into the chair, she heaved a large, wooden trunk with thick leather straps toward her. Charlotte unbuckled the straps and lifted the heavy lid. She was greeted by the smell of dusty fabric, mildew, age-old paper, and a scent that she couldn't quite place.

Rifling through the trunk's contents, Charlotte discovered some old baby clothes, a painting, and some books. Everything she picked up had charred edges, as if damaged by smoke and fire. That was the smell she couldn't place: smoke. From the very bottom of the trunk, she <u>procured</u> an old, leather-bound journal. Opening the cover, she read the writing on the first yellowed page. *Property of Mary Elizabeth Dushore*, the sprawling script read.

"I wonder who that is," mumbled Charlotte, as she flipped a few more pages to find the first entry. It was dated October 19, 1819:

> The happiness I feel today is greater than the happiness I felt on my wedding day, for
> Herbert and I have welcomed our daughter, Isabelle Marie, into the world. She's just shy
> of six pounds, with a head full of red hair and the tiniest fingers I've ever seen. She's the
> picture of perfection.

Charlotte twirled her own red hair around her finger as she flipped a few months further into the journal:

> January 1, 1820
>
> Happy New Year! I suppose that's the appropriate greeting for the New Year, but it seems
> that there's less to be happy about than usual. The weather's been dry as dust and showing
> no signs of letting up. Everyone in town is getting anxious about the lack of rain.

"Why was everyone so upset about a drought?" Charlotte wondered aloud. "Savannah's not exactly a rainforest."

"Who are you talking to?"

Startled by her mother's voice, Charlotte looked up and then waved the journal in the air.

"I'm just reading this lady's journal and wondering why everyone was so concerned about a drought."

Mrs. Mitchell sat down by her daughter and read the inscription on the inside cover.

"Do you know who 'this lady' is?" she asked.

Charlotte furrowed her brow as she searched the deep recesses of her brain to come up with a name, but nothing rang a bell.

"You remember Nana, your great-grandmother who died when you were about five years old," said Mrs. Mitchell.

Charlotte nodded.

"Well," Mrs. Mitchell continued, "Mary Elizabeth Dushore was Nana's great-great-grandmother, and her daughter, Isabelle, was Nana's great-grandmother."

Mrs. Mitchell instructed Charlotte to find the journal entry closest to January 11, 1820. Charlotte quickly scanned the pages, surprised to find the exact date her mother had mentioned, and even more astonished by the events described by Mary Elizabeth on that date:

> We're traveling now, on our way to stay with Herbert's parents in Virginia where Herbert's going to work for his uncle until he can save enough money to build a new house. The devastation back in Savannah is overwhelming. The dry conditions and wooden buildings were no match for the hungry flames of the fire. Herbert says that hundreds of structures were destroyed. I was able to snatch a few things from the house before we left, but many of our possessions were consumed by the fire. Thankfully, Herbert, Isabelle, and I escaped without a scratch and have a place to go. Some of our friends and neighbors were not quite so lucky.

Charlotte didn't realize that she had been holding her breath until she finally exhaled. She looked at her mother.

"Is our house the same one that Mary Elizabeth and Herbert rebuilt upon returning to Savannah?" she asked.

Mrs. Mitchell nodded as she surveyed the treasure trove of family history surrounding her daughter and herself.

"They returned to Savannah and built this house in 1825," said Mrs. Mitchell, "but Herbert and Mary Elizabeth never forgot what happened to them. When they returned to the city, Herbert volunteered his free time to fire departments, and Mary Elizabeth and he both taught people about fire prevention."

Charlotte closed the journal and returned it to its original location in the trunk. All the while she pondered what she had learned about her family's history. Later that night, as she helped her mother wash the dishes, she had a thought.

"Maybe I'll continue the family legacy and become a firefighter some day," she said.

"If you have half the courage and determination of our ancestors, I'm sure you'll be a great one," said Mrs. Mitchell, smiling at her daughter.

_Go On_

39. As used to describe Charlotte, the phrase "twirled her own red hair" is an example of which literary device?

   A. irony
   B. symbolism
   C. foreshadowing
   D. metaphor

40. The author's use of journal entries in the passage helps to create a tone that is

   A. nostalgic.
   B. mysterious.
   C. impersonal.
   D. sarcastic.

41. The author depicts Charlotte considering a career in firefighting at the end of the passage in order to show Charlotte's

   A. frustration.
   B. admiration.
   C. imagination.
   D. consternation.

42. Which sentence **best** describes the main idea of this passage?

   A. Charlotte attempts to clean the attic and gets sidetracked by the interesting things she finds.
   B. Charlotte's mother tells her daughter stories about how and when their house was built.
   C. Charlotte discovers a journal that reveals the bravery and strength of her ancestors.
   D. Charlotte's mother tries to help her daughter choose a challenging and rewarding career.

43. The phrase "nothing rang a bell" is an idiom for

   A. not recognizing something you should know.
   B. not hearing something the first time it's spoken.
   C. not being able to make an important decision.
   D. not asking for help when you need it most.

44. As used in the passage, the word <u>procured</u> **most** nearly means

    A. *uncovered.*
    B. *obtained.*
    C. *replaced.*
    D. *cleaned.*

45. Which statement from the passage **best** reflects the theme?

    A. "Rifling through the trunk's contents, Charlotte discovered some old baby clothes, a painting, and some books."
    B. "Charlotte furrowed her brow as she searched the deep recesses of her brain to come up with a name, but nothing rang a bell."
    C. "You remember Nana, your great-grandmother who died when you were about five years old."
    D. "If you have half the courage and determination of our ancestors, I'm sure you'll be a great one."

46. Suppose you are writing an essay about how violence on television affects teens. Which of the following is the **best** way to state your research question?

    A. What types of TV shows do teens consider the most interesting to watch?
    B. Does evidence suggest that watching violent TV shows leads to more teen violence?
    C. How much time do teens watch TV during an average week?
    D. What system do networks used to rate the amount of violence shown on TV shows?

47. Which of the following sentences is written correctly?

    A. Tamyra is the fastest runner of all.
    B. Tamyra is the more fast runner of all.
    C. Tamyra is the more faster runner of all.
    D. Tamyra is the fast runner of all.

Go On

Passage 7

Read the following passage and answer questions 48 through 54.

The Coolest Invention

When Willis Haviland Carrier invented his first cooling machine, he began a career that would eventually help millions of businesses and homes.

It often gets very hot during the summer. Long ago, few people could even bear to live in the southern United States because of the high temperatures. Many kinds of technology have been created since then to make hot climates more comfortable. Primary among these tools is the air conditioner.

We may take air conditioners for granted today, but they are very important to many aspects of modern life. Air conditioners don't just make our houses cool. They also help factories and businesses run efficiently year-round. They keep food, drinks, and medicine fresh and safe. They even protect paper from shrinking and film and paintings from warping.

People have tried to build cooling machines for well over a hundred years. The earliest air conditioners were giant pumps that sent dangerous chemicals through pipes. This did cause some cooling, but the toxic, *combustible* chemicals also caused poisoning and fires.

The first safe, modern air conditioner was invented by Willis Haviland Carrier in 1902. Just a year after completing his studies as an engineer, Carrier had a "flash of genius." While waiting for a train, he watched the fog and thought about humidity and temperature. By the time the train arrived, Carrier had figured out a formula that would allow a machine to control the temperature.

Go On

It was in 1902 that Carrier was hired to solve a big problem for a book publisher. The heat and humidity in the printing factory caused the paper to swell. The printers found it difficult to add different-colored inks to the pages because the pages kept warping. Carrier put his "flash of genius" to work and built the first air conditioner. Once installed in the factory, the air conditioner kept the temperature stable. The paper no longer warped. The publishers were thrilled with the device, and Carrier knew he had something special.

In 1906, Carrier revealed his perfected machine. The term *air conditioner* didn't catch on until later; at the time, Carrier called his invention the "Apparatus for Treating Air." Many industries purchased Carrier's machines, and in 1915, he went into business.

Carrier kept on improving his machines for use in factories and businesses. He didn't start thinking about keeping people cool until 1924, when he was asked to install his machines in a department store. Then, he installed some in movie theaters. People loved the technology and swarmed to whatever business featured the air-cooling devices.

The next great challenge for Carrier was creating an air conditioner that people could use in their homes. In 1928, he designed the "Weathermaker," a small, safe household unit. Over the following decades, thousands of people purchased Carrier's machines. Today, air conditioning is a staple in many homes and businesses—all thanks to Willis Haviland Carrier.

---

48. Which of the following was a problem with the first cooling machines?

   A. They created a fog.
   B. They heated too quickly.
   C. They were extremely loud.
   D. They used toxic chemicals.

49. According to this author, what was the cause of the problem faced by many book publishers?

   A. Their machines got too hot and had to be shut off.
   B. Heat and humidity damaged the paper they used.
   C. Workers in the factories got overheated very quickly.
   D. The different-colored inks ran into each other.

50. Which **best** describes the way in which the passage is structured?

   A. compare and contrast
   B. cause and effect
   C. problem and solution
   D. chronological order

Go On

51. As used in the passage, <u>combustible</u> **most** nearly means

    A. *moveable.*
    B. *flammable.*
    C. *perishable.*
    D. *uncontrollable.*

52. The author describes air conditioners saying,

They keep food, drinks, and medicine fresh and safe. They even protect paper from shrinking and film and paintings from warping.

The **most likely** reason the author chose these words would be to

    A imply that air conditioners consume a lot of energy.
    B. explain why Carrier invented the first safe air conditioner.
    C. demonstrate the importance of air conditioners to everyday life.
    D. suggest that better air conditioners are needed to keep things cool.

53. Which of these facts from the passage would be most relevant to use in a presentation detailing ways to boost sales at a store?

    A. People loved the technology and swarmed to whatever business featured the air-cooling devices.
    B. The first safe, modern air conditioner was invented by Willis Haviland Carrier in 1902.
    C. We may take air conditioners for granted today, but they are very important to many aspects of modern life.
    D. Over the following decades, thousands of people purchased Carrier's machines.

54. The **most likely** reason the author wrote this passage was to

    A. persuade readers to buy air conditioners.
    B. describe the hazards of early air conditioners.
    C. inform readers about the first air conditioners.
    D. discuss the life of the inventor of air conditioners.

Go On

Passage 8

Read the following passage and answer questions 55 through 60.

Excerpt from *Narrative of the Life of Frederick Douglass*

by Frederick Douglass

Frederick Douglass began his life as a slave, taught himself to read and write, and later became an eloquent speaker and a leader of the abolitionist movement to end slavery in the United States.

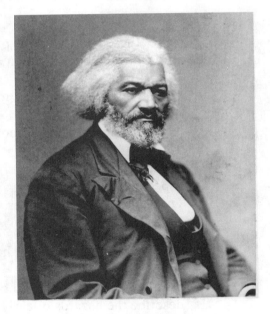

I was born in Tuckahoe, near Hillsborough, and about twelve miles from Easton, in Talbot County, Maryland. I have no accurate knowledge of my age, never having seen any authentic record containing it. By far the larger part of the slaves know as little of their ages as horses know of theirs, and it is the wish of most masters within my knowledge to keep their slaves thus ignorant. I do not remember to have ever met a slave who could tell of his birthday. They seldom come nearer to it than planting-time, harvest-time, cherry-time, spring-time, or fall-time. A want of information concerning my own was a source of unhappiness to me even during childhood. The white children could tell their ages. I could not tell why I ought to be deprived of the same privilege. I was not allowed to make any inquiries of my master concerning it. He deemed all such inquiries on the part of a slave improper and impertinent, and evidence of a restless spirit. The nearest estimate I can give makes me now between twenty-seven and twenty-eight years of age. I come to this, from hearing my master say, some time during 1835, I was about seventeen years old. . . .

My mother and I were separated when I was but an infant—before I knew her as my mother. It is a common custom, in the part of Maryland from which I ran away, to part children from their mothers at a very early age. Frequently, before the child has reached its twelfth month, its mother is taken from it, and hired out on some farm a considerable distance off, and the child is placed under the care of an old woman, too old for field labor. For what this separation is done, I do not

Go On

know, unless it be to hinder the development of the child's affection toward its mother, and to blunt and destroy the natural affection of the mother for the child. This is the inevitable result.

I never saw my mother, to know her as such, more than four or five times in my life; and each of these times was very short in duration, and at night. She was hired by a Mr. Stewart, who lived about twelve miles from my home. She made her journeys to see me in the night, travelling the whole distance on foot, after the performance of her day's work. She was a field hand, and a whipping is the penalty of not being in the field at sunrise, unless a slave has special permission from his or her master to the contrary—a permission which they seldom get, and one that gives to him that gives it the proud name of being a kind master. I do not recollect of ever seeing my mother by the light of day. She was with me in the night. She would lie down with me, and get me to sleep, but long before I waked she was gone. Very little communication ever took place between us. Death soon ended what little we could have while she lived, and with it her hardships and suffering. She died when I was about seven years old, on one of my master's farms, near Lee's Mill. I was not allowed to be present during her illness, at her death, or burial. She was gone long before I knew anything about it. Never having enjoyed, to any considerable extent, her soothing presence, her tender and watchful care, I received the tidings of her death with much the same emotions I should have probably felt at the death of a stranger. . . .

I have had two masters. My first master's name was Anthony. I do not remember his first name. He was generally called Captain Anthony—a title which, I presume, he acquired by sailing a craft on the Chesapeake Bay. He was not considered a rich slaveholder. He owned two or three farms, and about thirty slaves. His farms and slaves were under the care of an overseer. The overseer's name was Plummer. Mr. Plummer was a miserable drunkard, a profane swearer, and a savage monster. He always went armed with a cowskin and a heavy cudgel. I have known him to cut and slash the women's heads so horribly, that even master would be enraged at his cruelty, and would threaten to whip him if he did not mind himself. Master, however, was not a humane slaveholder. It required extraordinary barbarity on the part of an overseer to affect him. He was a cruel man, hardened by a long life of slaveholding. He would at times seem to take great pleasure in whipping a slave. . . . No words, no tears, no prayers, from his gory victim, seemed to move his iron heart from its bloody purpose. . . . It was a most terrible spectacle. I wish I could commit to paper the feelings with which I beheld it.

55. The point of view used in the passage reveals the author's

    A. joy after having escaped from slavery.
    B. pain over losing his mother as a boy.
    C. fear of being mistreated by his master.
    D. desire to return to his childhood home.

Go On

56. Which of the following conclusions can logically be drawn from the passage?

    A. The author escaped from the bonds of slavery.
    B. The author had a lot in common with his mother.
    C. Mr. Stewart was more successful than Captain Anthony.
    D. Most female slaves were not required to work in the fields.

57. The **most likely** reason the author wrote this passage was to

    A. persuade people to fight to end slavery.
    B. explain how people became slaves.
    C. describe what life was like for a slave.
    D. argue for better treatment of slaves.

58. Which assertion is **best** supported by the evidence in this passage?

    A. Masters on farms in Maryland were stricter than those further south.
    B. The author's mother knew that he would be mistreated by Mr. Plummer.
    C. Slaves were usually permitted to travel as long as they asked their masters.
    D. The author's mother loved him even though she couldn't care for him.

59. The author wrote,

It was a most terrible spectacle. I wish I could commit to paper the feelings with which I beheld it.

The **most likely** reason the author chose these words would be to

    A. show that he would like to discuss the mistreatment of slaves further.
    B. show that he is not permitted to discuss how horribly slaves were treated.
    C. imply that what he saw is something that he would like to forget.
    D. imply that words can't begin to describe the mistreatment of slaves.

60. This passage is an example of an autobiography because of its

    A. attention to the minute details of everyday life.
    B. depiction of events in the author's own life.
    C. focus on telling a story in rhythmic verse.
    D. description of a legendary or historical hero.

Stop

Georgia High School Writing Test

Practice Test 1

For the **Georgia High School Writing Test** (GHSWT) you will be given an answer book with a prompt inside. You will respond to a prompt that asks you to persuade.

The GHSWT is administered in one two-hour session. Ninety minutes of this session are used for student writing time. You will also use this time to edit and revise your writing. Your composition for this test will be no more than two pages in length.

Your composition should be written neatly and should show that you can organize and express your thoughts clearly and completely. You may not use a dictionary or other reference materials.

Writing Prompt

Writing Situation

A local parent has written a newspaper editorial on the subject of high school students with after-school jobs. He feels that after-school jobs are unnecessary for high school students, who are usually supported by their parents. He states that after-school jobs take time away from high school students' studies and are of no real value to the students.

Directions for Writing

Write an editorial for your local newspaper in response to this parent's editorial, in which you either agree or disagree with this parent's views on the value of after-school jobs. Clearly state your position. Try to convince readers of the paper to agree with you by providing well-developed supporting arguments.

Go On

Student Writing Checklist for Persuasive Writing[1]

Prepare yourself to write:

- [ ] Read the *Writing Situation* and *Directions for Writing* carefully.
- [ ] Brainstorm for ideas.
- [ ] Consider how to address your audience.
- [ ] Decide what ideas to include and how to organize them.
- [ ] Write only in English.

Make your paper meaningful:

- [ ] Use your knowledge and/or personal experiences that are related to the topic.
- [ ] Express a clear point of view.
- [ ] Fully support your argument with specific details, examples, and convincing reasons.
- [ ] Include an appeal to logic and/or emotions.
- [ ] Present your ideas in a clear and logical order.
- [ ] Stay on topic.

Make your paper interesting to read:

- [ ] Use examples and details that would be convincing to your audience.
- [ ] Use appropriate voice that shows your interest in the topic.
- [ ] Use precise, descriptive, vivid words.
- [ ] Vary the type, structure, and length of your sentences.
- [ ] Use effective transitions.

Edit and revise your paper:

- [ ] Consider rearranging your ideas and changing words to make your paper more effective.
- [ ] Add additional information or details to make your paper complete.
- [ ] Proofread your paper for usage, punctuation, capitalization, and spelling.

---

[1] Retrieved from *http://gadoe.org/_documents/curriculum/testing/ga_writing_assessment_ghswt.pdf*.

Stop

Answers

PT1 D   2   ELAALRL1.nonfiction.b

The author tells the reader that redwood trees are hard to describe and that they are "so large and beautiful that they take your breath away." The reader can conclude that there are few words that can truly capture the beauty of a redwood tree. None of the other assertions can be supported by the evidence in the passage.

1 C   3   ELA11C1

It is grammatically incorrect to say "the audition had gone good." Substituting the word *well* for the word *good* will make the sentence correct. *Good* is an adjective and an adjective modifies a noun. In this sentence, *good* is being used to modify the verb *had gone*. The word *well*, an adverb, is needed here.

2 B   3   ELA11C1

The quality of the school's lunches would have to be tested against the standards that are set up by the state government. Asking what the school board is doing to make lunches healthier, comparing the lunches to the lunches at other schools, or searching for a relationship between lunches and test scores does not tell you anything about the current quality of the lunches.

3 D   1   ELAALRL1.nonfiction.a

Ms. Anthony is addressing all of her fellow citizens. In doing this, she is showing her audience the absurdity of allowing only certain groups of citizens to vote when the United States Constitution gives this right to all citizens of the country.

4 A   1   ELAALRL1.nonfiction.a

Ms. Anthony states that it is her opinion that she did not break the law when she voted because she is a legal citizen of the United States. She follows this statement with details and quotes from the Declaration of Independence and the Unites States Constitution to support this claim.

5 C   2   ELAALRL1.nonfiction.c

Ms. Anthony uses examples from the Declaration of Independence and the United States Constitution to support her opinion that women, as citizens of the country, should have the right to vote.

6 B 2 ELAALRL1.nonfiction.c

Ms. Anthony gave this speech to show others that because women are citizens of the United States, held to the same laws as men, they should be able to vote in order to voice their opinions about laws and government.

7 C 1 ELAALRL5.a

As used in the speech, the word *organic* means *basic*. Ms. Anthony uses this word to show that the most fundamental rights are granted to all people, not a select few. This helps support her argument that there is no language in any of the "grand documents" that denies women the right to vote.

8 C 2 ELAALRL1.nonfiction.c

It is easy to see Ms. Anthony's frustration with the laws in place during her time. The other answer choices are not revealed when considering her point of view.

9 B 1 ELAALRL5.a

A *talisman* is a charm, meant to protect its bearer from jinxes and spells. Mercury gives this to Ulysses so he might be able to avoid being tricked by Circe and rescue his men.

10 D 2 ELAALRL1.fiction.a

The point of turning the men into pigs is to keep them on the island. Circe has never met Ulysses and there is no mention of Mercury before Circe casts her spell, making choices A and B incorrect. Circe doesn't seem concerned with the men's appearances (choice C), only that she has the power to capture and keep them on the island for her own amusement.

11 D 1 ELAALRL1.fiction.a

Ulysses tells the story as it happened, from first landing on the island to Circe telling him that he must journey to Hades before he can return home.

12 A 1 ELAALRL1.fiction.a

Ulysses never thinks about simply leaving his men behind, though he is aware of Circe's powers of trickery. Though it would be easier to continue without them, he goes to rescue them, showing that he is a loyal friend. The other answer choices do not apply.

13 C 1 ELAALRL1.fiction.d

The author says that Circe's voice is so beautiful that Polites wants to "see whether she is woman or goddess." He uses this language to show the reader that Circe's beautiful voice tricks the men into feeling secure. It is one of the many tools she uses to enchant the visitors that come to the island.

14 D 2 ELAALRL2.b

Mercury is sympathetic to Ulysses' problem. He calls Ulysses "my poor unhappy man" and tells him, "I will protect you and get you out of your difficulty." After saying this, Mercury gives Ulysses the talisman that protects him from Circe's enchantments.

15 C 2 ELAALRL1.fiction.c

The passage suggests that Ulysses was willing to do whatever it took to save his men, including risking his own life. By remaining loyal to his friends, he was able to save them.

16 A 3 ELA11C1

The word *passed* is the past tense of the verb *pass*. The word *past* refers to a period of time. The author meant to use *past* to show that Ryan was out *beyond* the time that he was supposed to be home.

17 B 3 ELA11C1

A semicolon is used to join two independent clauses to show the reader their relationship. The phrases "You better be home before nine" and "otherwise, you will be grounded" are independent clauses. A comma or a colon cannot join these two together.

18 D 1 ELAALRL1.poetry.a.ii

The poet says " 'Tis not love's going hurt my days. / But that it went in little ways." This means that she is not hoping that her lover returns, nor is she angry at him for leaving, but she is upset at the way that the relationship ended. There is also no evidence to support the idea that she wishes to escape her memories since most of the poem includes her memories of her "dear."

19 B 1 ELAALRL1.poetry.a.iii

Spring is often used as a symbol for the start of something. Spring is when flowers bloom and animals give birth. Here, the poet is using the season as a symbol for the beginning of her relationship. The images that she associates with spring, such as walking with her dear, show that the beginning of the relationship was happy. Fall is often used as a symbol for the end of something. Fall is the season when trees lose their leaves and animals go into hibernation. It is associated with dying, which is the final ending in all our lives. The poet uses negative images, such as the rooks trilling, in this part of the poem to show that the end of the relationship was an unhappy and dark time.

20 B 1 ELAALRL1.poetry.a.i

End rhyme occurs when words at the end of lines rhyme. The only correct example of this is answer choice B. While the words *wet* and *yet* (choice A) are rhyming words, only one of these words appears at the end of a line.

21 D 1 ELAALRL1.poetry.a.ii

Lyrical poems focus on the inner feelings of the speaker. This is an essential part of lyric poetry.

22 C 1 ELAALRL1.poetry.a.iii

The phrase "broke my heart in little ways" is an idiom. A person's heart cannot really "break." This saying just means that the poet experienced deep hurt, but her actual heart was still intact.

23 A 1 ELAALRL1.poetry.a.ii

The speaker repeats the images of spring and fall and compares and contrasts them to the beginning and end of a relationship.

24 C 2 ELAALRL1.nonfiction.c

The writer feels that though she did nothing wrong, she is being treated unfairly simply because she is a teenager. She is a little upset that her plans did not go the way she wanted them to, but the point of view mainly reveals that she feels unjustifiably stereotyped.

25 C 1 ELAALRL5.a

Commemorate means *celebrate*. The other answer choices do not fit the word as it was used in the paragraph.

26 D 2 ELAALRL1.nonfiction.c

The point of explaining her history with the movie theater is to show that she is a good customer who has never caused problems in the past. This helps the reader to understand why she feels that the curfew is unfair to teens that obey the rules.

27 C 2 ELAALRL1.nonfiction.c

The letter is addressed to the management office of the movie theater. The managers would be the only employees that could listen to Amber's concerns and possibly revise their curfew policies.

28 A 1 ELAALRL1.nonfiction.a

Though Amber is complaining about a problem and stating her opinion, much of the letter has to do with the retelling of what happened on the night of her birthday. This organizational pattern best describes how the letter is structured.

29 B 2 ELAALRL1.nonfiction.c

In the final paragraph, the writer expresses her desire to remain loyal to Merrymakers; however, she says that if the company does not reconsider their policy, she will have to take her business elsewhere. This hesitation gives the paragraph a reluctant feeling.

30 C 2 ELAALRL1.nonfiction.b

Amber's letter shows that some teenagers feel that certain rules, such as curfews at movie theaters, malls, and other stores, unfairly stereotype teens as troublemakers. These restrictions apply to teens who obey the rules, and many think that this is unfair.

31 C 3 ELA11C1

Items in a series should be separated by commas; answer choice C correctly adds these commas to the series of items that Tim is buying for the party. Adding the word *and* between each item or repeating the phrase *and buying* between each item is incorrect.

32 D 3 ELA11C1

No revision is needed in this passage. It is correct as is.

33 C 1 ELAALRL5.a

Using the context of the sentence and information in surrounding paragraphs, you can conclude that Sela is suffering from severe stage fright and is anxious about performing. Therefore, you can determine that *trepidation* and *anxiety* have nearly the same meaning.

34 B 2 ELAALRL1.fiction.c

This sentence represents the climax because it is the turning point in the story for Sela. Up to this point, Sela is nervous about performing and lacks confidence. After talking to Jules and learning that Jules looks up to her, Sela gains confidence in her musical talents and her stage fright begins to disappear.

35 D 1 ELAALRL1.fiction.d

The author describes Shaz's look as a "get-out-of-my-way-before-I-bite-you kind of gaze," which implies that she really has no fear of getting on stage.

36 B 1 ELAALRL1.fiction.a

Most of this story is dedicated to the internal conflict Sela has with her stage fright. However, this conflict is resolved when Sela finds out that Jules looks up to her as a confident and talented musician.

37 D 1 ELAALRL1.fiction.a

Similes make comparisons using *like* or *as*. In this case, Sela has amazing musical talents until she plays in front of someone. Then her talents disappear, or "vanish like a ghost."

38 B 1 ELAALRL1.fiction.a

When Jules reveals that she pretends to be Sela in order to overcome her stage fright, it is ironic because Sela has spent the whole story trying to find out how others deal with their stage fright. Meanwhile, she had the confidence and skill inside herself the whole time.

39 C 2 ELAALRL1.fiction.c

This phrase is placed right after Charlotte reads the journal entry in which Mary Elizabeth describes her daughter as having "a head full of red hair." By positioning the phrase here, the author foreshadows that Charlotte may be related to the woman who wrote the journal.

40 A 2 ELAALRL2.b

While there is a bit of mystery in the story, the tone of most of the story is nostalgic, or reflective about the past. Charlotte lives in a two-hundred-year-old house with an attic full of items from past generations and reads the journal of her great-grandmother's great-great-grandmother.

41 B 1 ELAALRL1.fiction.d

After Charlotte learns about the devastating fire and Herbert and Mary Elizabeth's dedication to firefighting and fire prevention, she is inspired to become a firefighter. This shows admiration for her ancestors.

42 C 1 ELAALRL1.fiction.a

The story is mainly about Charlotte's discovery of a journal that reveals how members of her family overcame a great tragedy, a devastating fire, only to build the house that she still lives in today.

43 A 1 ELAALRL5.a

When someone says that something "doesn't ring a bell" it means that it's unfamiliar to them. In this case, Charlotte can't place why the name Mary Elizabeth Dushore should be familiar to her.

44 B 1 ELAALRL5.a

The words *procured* and *obtained* are synonyms. Charlotte obtains the journal from the bottom of the trunk. The other words do not make sense within the context of the sentence.

45 D 2 ELAALRL1.fiction.c

Charlotte is inspired by Herbert and Mary Elizabeth, because even after they lost everything, they rebuilt and tried to help others. This sentence supports the idea that we can learn from those who lived before us.

46 B 3 ELA11C1

Answer choices A and C can be eliminated because they don't address how violence on television relates to teens. While answer choice D does discuss violence on television, it does not address how violence affects teens. Answer choice B is the best answer.

47 A 3 ELA11C1

Here, the superlative adjective *fastest* is comparing Tamyra to everyone else on the team and showing that she is the best.

48 D 2 ELAALRL1.nonfiction.b

The article says that the problem with the first cooling machine was that it used toxic chemicals that sometimes caused fires.

49 B 1 ELAALRL1.nonfiction.a

According to the author, heat and humidity caused the paper to warp. The warped paper did make it difficult to add different-colored inks to the paper, but the author never states that the colors ran together.

50 D 1 ELAALRL1.nonfiction.a

The passage does discuss the problems of earlier cooling machines, but its main purpose is to chronicle the events of Carrier's career from the invention of his first cooling machine to the home units he created many years later.

51 B 1 ELAALRL5.a

Using context clues, you can determine that combustible chemicals cause fires. Therefore, you should realize that *combustible* and *flammable* are synonyms.

52 C 2 ELAALRL1.nonfiction.c

The author likely chose these words to show the variety of things that air conditioners help to keep cool. By listing the items this way, the author shows how important air conditioners have become.

53 A 2 ELAALRL1.nonfiction.b

If people wanted to boost sales at a store, it would be relevant to tell them that places with air conditioners receive more businesses than those without them.

54 C 2 ELAALRL1.nonfiction.c

While the author does discuss hazards associated with early air conditioners, the majority of the passage tells about the invention of the first air conditioners and how they gradually improved over time.

55 C 1 ELAALRL1.fiction.a

Douglass explained that he couldn't find the words to describe how awful it was to see slaves being whipped by their masters. This reveals his own fear of being mistreated by his master.

56 A 2 ELAALRL1.nonfiction.c

Douglass's comment in paragraph 2, "It is a common custom, in the part of Maryland from which I ran away," implies that he eventually escaped from slavery.

57 C 2 ELAALRL1.nonfiction.c

While the author argued against slavery later in his life, his main purpose here is describing what life was like for slaves. Having been a slave himself, he offers a firsthand account of the slave experience.

58 D 2 ELAALRL1.nonfiction.b

Douglass's mother risked being whipped by her master when she came to visit her son. This shows that even though he received most of his care from someone else, his mother was still concerned about his well-being and loved him.

59 D 2 ELAALRL1.nonfiction.c

By saying that he wishes he could put feelings on paper, the author implies that he would describe the horrors of slavery if he could, but he can't find the right words to express how terrible it was.

60 B 1 ELAALRL1.nonfiction.a

An autobiography is the story of a person's life told by that person instead of by another author.

Writing Sample Answer

I think that after-school jobs are valuable for high school students for a number of reasons. First, I think that seeking an after-school job gives students a taste of what it is like to seek a full-time job. Students must first hunt down a job opportunity through the use of a newspaper or through word of mouth. They must then request, fill out, and submit an application for the desired position. If a student is called for an interview, he or she will then experience the interview process. This is a valuable skill, as most adults must take these same steps when seeking full-time employment. A student who has had even limited experience in this process is far more prepared to seek employment after graduation than one who has not.

Another reason that holding a part-time job is valuable for high school students is that it gives them experience in completing necessary tasks and taking orders from authority figures outside of the home environment. Many high school-age children become accustomed to rebelling against parental requests and orders, even when completing the simplest tasks around the home. Often, this rebellion is met with only mild repercussions; most punishments for bad behavior at home involve the removal of certain privileges for a short amount of time. Young adults need to learn that their actions can have serious repercussions in the real world. Holding a part-time job can teach them that they must respect and submit to authority figures, because many adults with full-time jobs must do the same on a daily basis.

Finally, holding a part-time job introduces the ideas of financial independence and responsibility. A young adult can achieve a great sense of satisfaction in earning his or her own paychecks. This also weans children away from their financial dependence on their parents and teaches them how to decide which expenses are important at the time. The most financially conscious students may choose to save their income, another valuable skill that translates into real-world success. For these reasons, I feel that holding part-time jobs can be very beneficial to high-school students.

Georgia High School Graduation Test

ELA Practice Test 2

Read the passage and answer the question that follows.

Bird Brains

Do animals have the capacity to retain as much information as human beings? This question has been presented by scientists for many years. To properly answer it, one scientist decided to ask an animal with speech capabilities: the African gray parrot.

In the late 1970s, research scientist Irene Pepperberg set out to prove that African gray parrots have cognitive abilities. Dr. Pepperberg has worked with a specific parrot named Alex for more than twenty-eight years. Her research has sparked much debate within the scientific community.

Alex can name more than fifty different objects when they are presented to him. He can express certain desires and accept or refuse the requests of others. Alex can answer questions about the colors, shapes, and materials of different objects with approximately 80 percent accuracy. He can make comparisons and sort items by type. Alex can also count up to six and find hidden items.

While Dr. Pepperberg acknowledges that the brains of these birds are far different from the human brain, her experiments prove that African gray parrots can think and feel in ways that are similar to human thought processes and emotions.

PT1 Which of these facts from the passage would be most useful to use in a presentation about zoology and human nature?

    A. Dr. Pepperberg is a research scientist who works with birds.
    B. Alex can recognize more than fifty objects when shown to him.
    C. African gray parrots think and feel in ways similar to humans.
    D. Dr. Pepperberg has worked with Alex for over twenty years.

Read the following passage and answer question 1.

Before traveling to her track meet, Joyce ate her usual breakfast; an orange, a bowl of bran flakes with skim milk, and a banana.

1. What revision, if any, is needed to the passage?

   A. Change *traveling* to *traveling*.
   B. Change the semicolon after *breakfast* to a colon.
   C. Change *breakfast* to *brakefast*.
   D. No correction is needed.

2. Which sentence would be **best** to include in a letter to the school principal requesting a longer lunch period?

   A. The lunch period is so brief that we can't get our homework done before class.
   B. My lunch period is over long before I finish talking with my friends.
   C. The lunch period ends before we have a chance to clean up after ourselves.
   D. Lunch period ends so fast, there's hardly any time to listen to my voicemail.

Passage 1

Read the following poem and answer questions 3 through 8.

in Just-

by e.e. cummings

in Just-
spring when the world is mud-
luscious the little
lame balloonman

whistles far and wee

and eddieandbill come
running from marbles and
piracies and it's
spring

when the world is puddle-wonderful

the queer
old balloonman whistles
far and wee
and bettyandisbel come dancing

from hop-scotch and jump-rope and

it's
spring
and
the

goat-footed

balloonMan whistles
far
and
wee

Go On

3. The writer is **most likely** trying to convey

    A. the sound of dancing.
    B. the feeling of spring.
    C. the rules of games.
    D. the smell of rain.

4. Which phrase from the poem is an example of alliteration?

    A. "luscious the little lame balloonman"
    B. "and eddieandbill come running"
    C. "marbles and piracies and it's spring"
    D. "from hop-scotch and jump-rope"

5. This poem is **most** like

    A. a ballad.
    B. a sonnet.
    C. free verse.
    D. blank verse.

6. This poem is an example of the literary movement postmodernism because of its

    A. disregard for the natural world.
    B. fragmentary organization of ideas.
    C. measured rhyme, rhythm, and meter.
    D. acceptance of the idea of absolute truth.

7. In the poem, cummings **most likely** uses the words *eddieandbill* and *bettyandisbel* in order to

    A. suggest the children's frustration.
    B. show that they're the same people.
    C. suggest the children's breathlessness.
    D. show that they don't like balloonman.

8. As used to describe the setting, the phrase "puddle-wonderful" is an example of which literary device?

    A. hyperbole
    B. symbolism
    C. metonymy
    D. paradox

Go On

Passage 2

Read the following passage and answer questions 9 through 15.

The Carbohydrate Craze

Dr. Rubina Gad

In this essay, Dr. Rubina Gad explains the current, popular nutritional ideas about carbohydrates. She attempts to debunk myths about the healthiness of carbohydrates and teach readers to consume healthy amounts of carbohydrates.

The American public's obsession with dieting has led to one of the most dangerous health misconceptions of all time. Many television ads, sitcoms, movies, magazine articles, and diet-food product labels would have consumers believe that carbohydrates are bad for the human body and that those who eat them will quickly become overweight. We are advised to avoid foods such as pasta, potatoes, rice, and white bread and opt for meats and vegetables instead. Some companies promote this idea to encourage consumers to buy their "carb-free" food products. But the truth is, as I stress to patients who come to our weight-loss clinic, the human body needs carbohydrates to function properly, and a body that is starved of this dietary element is not in good shape after all.

Carbohydrates are macronutrients, meaning they are essential sources of fuel that are necessary for survival. Contrary to popular belief, carbohydrates have many health benefits; however, the key to maintaining a healthy body is to consume these and other macronutrients—such as protein and fat—in appropriate amounts.

Most foods that we consume on a daily basis are loaded with carbohydrates. Many people mistakenly believe that carbohydrates can only be found in filling foods such as potatoes and pastas. In truth, carbohydrates are also naturally found in fruits, vegetables, dairy products, and whole grains. Many of these carbohydrate-containing foods also have essential health benefits; some fight diseases such as high blood pressure and heart disease, and others help to prevent cancer and stroke. Cutting these foods out of your diet may increase your chances of contracting one of these diseases. It also deprives your body of the many health benefits of carbohydrates.

One of the best benefits of carbohydrates is their ability to provide fuel to the muscles and the brain. They also help to maintain the health of our organs, tissues, and cells. Scientific studies have shown that one type of carbohydrate called fiber, also commonly referred to as roughage, reduces the risk of heart disease and diabetes. Carbohydrates also contain antioxidants, which protect the body's cells from harmful particles with the potential to cause cancer.

This does not mean that the human body can survive on a diet composed entirely of carbohydrates. We also need certain percentages of proteins and fats to maintain healthy bodies.

Go On

But carbohydrates certainly should not be avoided altogether. In fact, the food pyramid, the recommended basis for a healthy diet, shows that a person should consume six to eleven servings of breads, grains, and pastas, as well as three to four servings each of fruits and vegetables—all carbohydrate-containing foods. It is easy to see why cutting carbohydrates out of a person's diet is not a good idea.

The only way to know what is truly healthy for your own body is to talk to a nutritionist or dietitian, who can help you choose foods that are right for you as well as guide you toward a proper exercise program for weight loss, muscle gain, or toning. These professionals will never tell you to cut out carbohydrates entirely. The bottom line: listen to the experts, not the advertisers!

9. As used in the passage, <u>misconceptions</u> **most** nearly means

   A. *historical events.*
   B. *wrong beliefs.*
   C. *huge disasters.*
   D. *health epidemics.*

Go On

10. Which sentence from the passage **best** reflects the main idea?

    A. "The human body needs carbohydrates to function properly."
    B. "Carbohydrates are macronutrients, essential sources of fuel."
    C. "Carbohydrates are in fruits, vegetables, and dairy products."
    D. "Professionals will never tell you to cut out carbohydrates."

11. Which **best** describes the way in which the passage is structured?

    A. a conflict followed by a resolution
    B. main idea with personal anecdotes
    C. list of details proving an assertion
    D. chronological sequence of events

12. Which assertion is **best** supported by the evidence in the passage?

    A. You should eat many different kinds of food.
    B. You might get sick without enough protein.
    C. Too many carbohydrates will make you tired.
    D. Carbohydrates are found in meat and poultry.

13. What is the **most likely** reason readers should believe the author about carbohydrates?

    A. She has talked to nutritionists.
    B. She works at a weight-loss clinic.
    C. She has studied the food pyramid.
    D. She conducts a lot of research.

14. As used in the passage, contracting **most** nearly means

    A. *immunizing.*
    B. *doing work.*
    C. *making a deal.*
    D. *acquiring.*

Go On

15. What is an effect of cutting carbohydrates out of your diet, according to this author?

    A. Your risk of heart disease and diabetes will decrease.
    B. Your body will miss getting many antioxidants.
    C. You'll lower your chances of having a stroke.
    D. Your body will get in much better shape.

16. Which of the sentences below is written correctly?

    A. Let's spend fewer hours talking, and more hours doing.
    B. Lets spend few hours talking, and more hours doing.
    C. Lets spend lesser hours talking, and more hours doing.
    D. Let's spend less hours talking, and more hours doing.

17. Which sentence would be **best** to include in a letter to the president of the United States commenting on current politics?

    A. According to all the television news I watch, you're doing a good job.
    B. When I read the paper this morning, I saw the best cartoon about you.
    C. As a student and citizen, I do appreciate your dedication to our nation.
    D. When I saw the shirt you wore to the benefit, I just had to write to you.

Go On

Passage 3

Read the following passage and answer questions 18 through 23.

Departure

by Sherwood Anderson

In this short story from the novel Winesburg, Ohio, George Willard is leaving the town he's lived in his entire life.

Young George Willard got out of bed at four in the morning. It was April and the young tree leaves were just coming out of their buds. The trees along the residence streets in Winesburg are maple and the seeds are winged. When the wind blows they whirl crazily about, filling the air and making a carpet underfoot.

George came downstairs into the hotel office carrying a brown leather bag. His trunk was packed for departure. Since two o'clock he had been awake thinking of the journey he was about to take and wondering what he would find at the end of his journey. The boy who slept in the hotel office lay on a cot by the door. His mouth was open and he snored lustily. George crept past the cot and went out into the silent deserted main street. The east was pink with the dawn and long streaks of light climbed into the sky where a few stars still shone.

Beyond the last house on Trunion Pike in Winesburg there is a great stretch of open fields. The fields are owned by farmers who live in town and drive homeward at evening along Trunion Pike in light creaking wagons. In the fields are planted berries and small fruits. In the late afternoon in the hot summers when the road and the fields are covered with dust, a smoky haze lies over the great flat basin of land. To look across it is like looking out across the sea. In the spring when the land is green the effect is somewhat different. The land becomes a wide green billiard table on which tiny human insects toil up and down.

All through his boyhood and young manhood George Willard had been in the habit of walking on Trunion Pike. He had been in the midst of the great open place on winter nights when it was covered with snow and only the moon looked down at him; he had been there in the fall when bleak winds blew and on summer evenings when the air <u>vibrated</u> with the song of insects. On the April morning he wanted to go there again, to walk again in the silence. He did walk to where the road dipped down by a little stream two miles from town and then turned and walked silently back again. When he got to Main Street clerks were sweeping the sidewalks before the stores. "Hey, you George. How does it feel to be going away?" they asked.

The westbound train leaves Winesburg at seven forty-five in the morning. Tom Little is conductor. His train runs from Cleveland to where it connects with a great trunk line railroad with terminals in Chicago and New York. Tom has what in railroad circles is called an "easy run."

Go On

Every evening he returns to his family. In the fall and spring he spends his Sundays fishing in Lake Erie. He has a round red face and small blue eyes. He knows the people in the towns along his railroad better than a city man knows the people who live in his apartment building.

George came down the little incline from the New Willard House at seven o'clock. Tom Willard carried his bag. The son had become taller than the father.

On the station platform everyone shook the young man's hand. More than a dozen people waited about. Then they talked of their own affairs. Even Will Henderson, who was lazy and often slept until nine, had got out of bed. George was embarrassed. Gertrude Wilmot, a tall thin woman of fifty who worked in the Winesburg post office, came along the station platform. She had never before paid any attention to George. Now she stopped and put out her hand. In two words she voiced what everyone felt. "Good luck," she said sharply and then turning went on her way.

When the train came into the station George felt relieved. He scampered hurriedly aboard. Helen White came running along Main Street hoping to have a parting word with him, but he had found a seat and did not see her. When the train started Tom Little punched his ticket, grinned and, although he knew George well and knew on what adventure he was just setting out, made no comment. Tom had seen a thousand George Willards go out of their towns to the city. It was a commonplace enough incident with him. In the smoking car there was a man who had just invited Tom to go on a fishing trip to Sandusky Bay. He wanted to accept the invitation and talk over details.

George glanced up and down the car to be sure no one was looking, then took out his pocket-book and counted his money. His mind was occupied with a desire not to appear green. Almost the last words his father had said to him concerned the matter of his behavior when he got to the city. "Be a sharp one," Tom Willard had said. "Keep your eyes on your money. Be awake. That's the ticket. Don't let anyone think you're a greenhorn."

After George counted his money he looked out of the window and was surprised to see that the train was still in Winesburg.

The young man, going out of his town to meet the adventure of life, began to think but he did not think of anything very big or dramatic. Things like his mother's death, his departure from Winesburg, the uncertainty of his future life in the city, the serious and larger aspects of his life did not come into his mind.

He thought of little things—Turk Smollet wheeling boards through the main street of his town in the morning, a tall woman, beautifully gowned, who had once stayed overnight at his father's hotel, Butch Wheeler the lamp lighter of Winesburg hurrying through the streets on a summer evening and holding a torch in his hand, Helen White standing by a window in the Winesburg post office and putting a stamp on an envelope.

The young man's mind was carried away by his growing passion for dreams. One looking at him would not have thought him particularly sharp. With the recollection of little things occupying his mind he closed his eyes and leaned back in the car seat. He stayed that way for a long time and when he aroused himself and again looked out of the car window the town of Winesburg had disappeared and his life there had become but a background on which to paint the dreams of his manhood.

Go On

18. The phrase "To look across it is like looking out across the sea" is a simile for

    A. how dark the fields are at night.
    B. how the smoke is flat and wide.
    C. how wet the fields are at night.
    D. how the smoke comes in waves.

19. According to the passage, how does Tom Little feel about George leaving Winesburg?

    A. He is indifferent to George's going.
    B. He is delighted that George is leaving.
    C. He is jealous that George is going.
    D. He is depressed to see George leaving.

20. The author depicts George's behavior when he is alone in the car in order to show that George

    A. hasn't brought enough money for his trip.
    B. is nervous about leaving his hometown.
    C. thinks Tom took too much of his money.
    D. is tired and wants to sleep on the train.

21. According to the context of the fourth paragraph, <u>vibrated</u> means

    A. *offended.*
    B. *hesitated.*
    C. *trembled.*
    D. *hummed.*

22. This passage illustrates which theme from American literature?

    A. The American Dream leads to loneliness.
    B. Diversity is vastly important to success.
    C. The group tries to control the individual.
    D. Americans long to explore the unknown.

23. Throughout the story, Anderson characterizes George Willard to suggest that

    A. George wishes he didn't have to leave the small town.
    B. George wants to make the town better for its inhabitants.
    C. George wants to remember the small town when he leaves.
    D. George wishes more people would have come to see him off.

Go On

Passage 4

Read the following passage and answer questions 24 through 30.

College-Bound Turnaround

In her diary, Carrie, a high-school student about to graduate, contemplates making a life-changing decision.

Dear Diary,

It's amazing how quickly life can change sometimes! Before this week, I never imagined that I would want to attend college. I spent my whole life thinking that I would start working at a full-time job as soon as I graduated from high school. I imagined myself gaining some experience at that job and then hopefully being promoted into a managerial position that I could hold for many years.

My parents always wanted me to go to college, but they gave me the freedom to make my own choices. And my choice was: No college for me! I never gave any other possibility a second thought.

This week, though, Adrian came home to stay with us over winter break. She has been attending Bruni University, where she is majoring in art education. Although she's my sister—and a great sister, at that—I never really stopped to think about the things she does with her time, or what her life in college is like. I realized I'd been so wrapped up in myself I lost track of what Adrian was doing.

On Saturday, I asked Adrian about her college experience. She was very happy to share what she knew. Adrian told the whole family many stories about her classes and friends and the many things she's learned. She also told us how much she enjoys college and how she was actually eager to return to school after break. I found this hard to believe, since I never liked school. But maybe, I thought, I'd just never given it a chance.

Before Adrian left, she asked me if I wanted to come to Bruni for a visit. Since I was still on break from school, I followed her back to the university. I never thought that short trip would change my mind about college.

Adrian took me on a tour of the campus, and I was very impressed. Many things about the university appealed to me. The buildings were old and unique, and the campus was full of trees and sunny, <u>tranquil</u> spots to study. While we were walking around, I met some of Adrian's friends. They were all very nice to me, and I could tell that they thought my sister was a talented artist.

Adrian told her friends that I was a very good writer, which embarrassed me, but it also made me reflect on who I am and what I want to do. Suddenly I thought about how fun it would be to expand upon my own interests and talents—and I worried that a full-time job might not encourage me to do that. When we got back to Adrian's apartment, I started looking at the university's catalog. I saw that they offered a lot of different writing classes that sounded both fun and interesting.

That was the story of my trip to Bruni University, but it's also the story behind one of my life's biggest decisions: I've decided I want to attend college after graduation! I'm even going to take a writing workshop this summer. I would say I owe it all to my sister, but really the change came from inside of me. Maybe that's what getting older is all about.

Carrie

---

24. As used in the passage, <u>tranquil</u> **most** nearly means

A. *ugly.*
B. *nervous.*
C. *peaceful.*
D. *faraway.*

25. Which statement from the passage **best** reflects the theme?

A. "It's amazing how quickly things change sometimes!"
B. "She was very happy to share what she knew."
C. "But maybe, I thought, I'd just never given it a chance."
D. "And my choice was: No college for me!"

26. The author talks about meeting Adrian's friends on campus in order to show the students'

A. quantity.
B. skills.
C. uncertainty.
D. friendliness.

Go On

27. The point of view used in the passage reveals

    A. the narrator's reliance on her parents.
    B. the narrator's excitement about her idea.
    C. Adrian's enjoyment of high school life.
    D. Adrian's reluctance to help Carrie.

28. Which **best** describes the way in which the passage is structured?

    A. details describing a setting
    B. a claim with arguments
    C. a sequence of events
    D. conflict followed by resolution

29. The author writes that "the change came from inside of me." The **most likely** reason the author chose these words would be to

    A. suggest that she did not feel the change was a good idea.
    B. reveal that she did not carefully think about the change.
    C. explain that the change was almost entirely her decision.
    D. try to give Adrian credit for urging her to make a change.

30. In the diary entry, the author opens with a statement about life in order to

    A. introduce the important decision she made.
    B. show that she has a new understanding of her sister.
    C. explain how her life used to be when she was younger.
    D. describe ways in which her family has changed.

31. Which sentence would be **best** to include in a letter to a prospective employer requesting an interview for a position as a college professor's assistant?

    A. Because I have rarely been fired, you should really hire me.
    B. Because of all my babysitting experience, kids really like me.
    C. I pride myself on always being professional, punctual, and polite.
    D. This job seems good, but in time I'll seek a better-paying position.

Go On

Read the following passage and answer question 32.

Carl packed a picnic for all seven of us; however, Marie said the clam chowder he made was too salty.

32. What revision, if any, is needed to the passage?

A. Change *packed* to *pact*.
B. Change the semicolon after *us* to a comma.
C. Change *however* to *However*.
D. No correction is needed.

Go On

Passage 5

Read the following passage and answer questions 33 through 38.

A Wagner Matinee

by Willa Cather

"A Wagner Matinee" was written by twentieth-century novelist Willa Cather. In this story, narrator Clark Hamilton has moved to Boston and left behind all traces of rural Nebraska, where he was raised. When his aunt comes to visit him in the city, he takes her to a matinee, and she hears music for the first time in many years.

I received one morning a letter, written in pale ink on glassy, blue-lined notepaper, and bearing the postmark of a little Nebraska village. This communication . . . was from my Uncle Howard and informed me that his wife had been left a small legacy by a bachelor relative who had recently died. . . . It would be necessary for her to go to Boston to attend to the settling of the estate. He requested me to meet her at the station and render her whatever services might be necessary. . . .

When the train arrived I had some difficulty in finding my aunt. She was the last of the passengers to alight, and it was not until I got her into the carriage that she seemed really to recognize me. She had come all the way in a day coach; her linen duster had become black with soot, and her black bonnet gray with dust, during the journey. . . .

My Aunt Georgiana had been a music teacher at the Boston Conservatory, somewhere back in the latter sixties. One summer, while visiting in the little village among the Green Mountains where her ancestors had dwelt for generations, she had kindled the callow fancy of the most idle and shiftless of all the village lads. . . . The upshot of this <u>inexplicable</u> infatuation was that she eloped with him, eluding the reproaches of her family and the criticisms of her friends by going with him to the Nebraska frontier. Carpenter, who, of course, had no money, had taken a homestead in Red Willow County, fifty miles from the railroad. . . . For thirty years my aunt had not been further than fifty miles from the homestead. . . .

I owed to this woman most of the good that ever came my way in my boyhood, and had a reverential affection for her. During the years when I was riding herd for my uncle, my aunt, after cooking the three meals . . . would often stand until midnight at her ironing board, with me at the kitchen table beside her, hearing me recite Latin declensions and conjugations, gently shaking me when my drowsy head sank down over a page of irregular verbs. It was to her, at her ironing or mending, that I read my first Shakespeare', and her old textbook on mythology was the first that ever came into my empty hands.

She taught me my scales and exercises, too—on the little parlor organ, which her husband had bought her after fifteen years. . . .

Go On

When my aunt appeared on the morning after her arrival she was still in a semi-somnambulant state. . . . I had planned a little pleasure for her that afternoon, to repay her for some of the glorious moments she had given me when we used to milk together in the straw-thatched cowshed and she, because I was more than usually tired, or because her husband had spoken sharply to me, would tell me of the splendid performance of the *Huguenots* she had seen in Paris, in her youth. At two o'clock the Symphony Orchestra was to give a Wagner program, and I intended to take my aunt; though, as I conversed with her I grew doubtful about her enjoyment of it. Indeed, for her own sake, I could only wish her taste for such things quite dead, and the long struggle mercifully ended at last. . . . She was chiefly concerned that she had forgotten to leave instructions about feeding half-skimmed milk to a certain weakling calf, "old Maggie's calf, you know, Clark," she explained, evidently having forgotten how long I had been away. . . .

I asked her whether she had ever heard any of the Wagnerian operas and found that she had not. . . . I began to think it would have been best to get her back to Red Willow County without waking her, and regretted having suggested the concert.

From the time we entered the concert hall, however, she was a trifle less passive and inert, and for the first time seemed to perceive her surroundings. I had felt some trepidation lest she might become aware of the absurdities of her attire, or might experience some painful embarrassment at stepping suddenly into the world to which she had been dead for a quarter of a century. . . .

When the musicians came out and took their places, she gave a little stir of anticipation and looked with quickening interest down over the rail at that invariable grouping, perhaps the first wholly familiar thing that had greeted her eye since she had left old Maggie and her weakling calf. I could feel how all those details sank into her soul, for I had not forgotten how they had sunk into mine when I came fresh from plowing forever and forever between green aisles of corn, where, as in a treadmill, one might walk from daybreak to dusk without perceiving a shadow of change. I recalled how, in the first orchestra I had ever heard, those long bow strokes seemed to draw the heart out of me. . . .

When the horns drew out the first strain of the Pilgrim's chorus my Aunt Georgiana clutched my coat sleeve. Then it was I first realized that for her this broke a silence of thirty years; the inconceivable silence of the plains. . . .

The overture closed; my aunt released my coat sleeve, but she said nothing. . . . What, I wondered, did she get from it? She had often told me of Mozart's operas and Meyerbeer's, and I could remember hearing her sing, years ago, certain melodies of Verdi's. When I had fallen ill with a fever in her house she used to sit by my cot in the evening—when the cool, night wind blew in through the faded mosquito netting tacked over the window, and I lay watching a certain bright star that burned red above the cornfield—and sing "Home to our mountains, O, let us return!" in a way fit to break the heart of a Vermont boy near dead of homesickness already.

I watched her closely through the prelude to *Tristan and Isolde* . . . but she sat mutely staring at the violin bows that drove obliquely downward, like the pelting streaks of rain in a summer shower. Had this music any message for her?

. . . Soon after the tenor began the "Prize Song," I heard a quick drawn breath and turned to my aunt. Her eyes were closed, but the tears were glistening on her cheeks, and I think, in a moment more, they were in my eyes as well. It never really died, then—the soul that can suffer so excruciatingly and so interminably; it withers to the outward eye only; like that strange moss which can lie on a dusty shelf half a century and yet, if placed in water, grows green again. . . .

Go On

Her lip quivered and she hastily put her handkerchief up to her mouth. From behind it she murmured, "And you have been hearing this ever since you left me, Clark?" Her question was the gentlest and saddest of reproaches.

My aunt wept quietly, but almost continuously, as a shallow vessel overflows in a rainstorm. From time to time her dim eyes looked up at the lights which studded the ceiling, burning softly under their dull glass globes; doubtless they were stars in truth to her. I was still perplexed as to what measure of musical comprehension was left to her, she who had heard nothing but the singing of gospel hymns at Methodist services in the square frame schoolhouse on Section Thirteen for so many years. I was wholly unable to gauge how much of it had been dissolved in soapsuds, or worked into bread, or milked into the bottom of a pail.

The concert was over; the people filed out of the hall chattering and laughing, glad to relax and find the living level again, but my kinswoman made no effort to rise. The harpist slipped its green felt cover over his instrument; the flute players shook the water from their mouthpieces; the men of the orchestra went out one by one, leaving the stage to the chairs and music stands, empty as a winter cornfield.

I spoke to my aunt. She burst into tears and sobbed pleadingly. "I don't want to go, Clark, I don't want to go!"

I understood. For her, just outside the door of the concert hall, lay the black pond with the cattle-tracked bluffs; the tall, unpainted house, with weather-curled boards; naked as a tower, the crook-backed ash seedlings where the dishcloths hung to dry; the gaunt, molting turkeys picking up refuse about the kitchen door.

---

33. The language in this passage creates a tone that is

A. reflective.
B. objective.
C. humorous.
D. resentful.

Go On

Read this sentence from the passage and answer the question below.

> One summer, while visiting in the little village among the Green Mountains where her ancestors had dwelt for generations, she had kindled the callow fancy of the most idle and shiftless of all the village lads.

34. The author is **most likely** trying to convey that

    A. many people noticed the girl.
    B. many people were inspired by the girl.
    C. the girl dressed in very elegant clothes.
    D. the girl was incredibly social.

35. What is the **most likely** reason the narrator regrets having suggested the concert to his aunt?

    A. She seems very tired and wants to rest.
    B. She is in a hurry to go back to the farm.
    C. She seems to have forgotten such things.
    D. She looks improper because of her clothing.

36. What does Aunt Georgiana realize in the story?

    A. She truly misses her life on the farm.
    B. She has missed listening to music.
    C. She has lost the love of her nephew.
    D. She wants to play piano again.

37. The metaphor "that strange moss which can lie on a dusty shelf half a century" compares the love of music to

    A. a plant that can't seem to flower.
    B. a plant that can come back to life.
    C. a plant that never loses its bloom.
    D. a plant that has dried up and died.

38. As used in the passage, <u>inexplicable</u> **most** nearly means

    A. *doomed to disaster.*
    B. *accidental.*
    C. *destined to happen.*
    D. *mysterious.*

Go On

Passage 6

Read the following passage and answer questions 39 through 45.

The Battle of Chickamauga

Considered one of the worst battles of the Civil War, the Battle of Chickamauga featured brave fighting and strategic movements of both Union and Confederate soldiers.

The Civil War was a conflict that stretched across vast amounts of North America. Although most of the fighting was centered in Virginia, battles raged throughout the southeastern states. Georgia was the scene of one of the war's climactic clashes—the Battle of Chickamauga.

In 1862, Union and Confederate armies were busy fighting for control of Tennessee. Even after a number of bloody battles, neither side had gained a clear advantage. The armies retired to their camps for the winter while their commanders planned new maneuvers for the coming year.

By the summer of 1863, Union General William S. Rosecrans had his strategy ready. Leading his troops, the Army of the Cumberland, he marched out to do battle in Tennessee again. His target was the Confederate Army of Tennessee, led by General Braxton Bragg.

General Bragg expected that Rosecrans was preparing to attack near Knoxville, a major city in Tennessee. Losing control of Knoxville would be a disaster for the Confederate armies, so Bragg moved quickly to fortify the city. However, Bragg soon realized that he'd been deceived. Rosecrans had actually moved the Union army into the south, below Knoxville, right into northwestern Georgia. He was heading toward Atlanta—a city that was absolutely crucial to the Southern cause—instead of Knoxville.

Bragg again had to move rapidly, this time southward. His Army of Tennessee raced the Army of the Cumberland into Georgia. At first it looked as though General Rosecrans would be the ultimate victor, but the tides soon turned against him. The Union army faced a long, hard march over rugged mountains. Their progress was slowed even further by numerous attacks by the small Confederate units they encountered along the way. In order to deal with both the poor roads and the stubborn opposition, the army had to divide into smaller groups.

Meanwhile, General Bragg was faring much better. Other Confederate armies joined his army to help stop the Union advance. Among these armies were soldiers from Tennessee, Mississippi, and Virginia. The Virginian troops were commanded by General James Longstreet, one of the greatest generals in the South. Bragg gathered his troops and rushed to attack the divided Union armies before they could reunite.

On September 18, 1863, Bragg marched out to attack part of the Union army along Chickamauga Creek in northwestern Georgia. *Chickamauga* is a Native American word meaning *Stagnant River*, but, after the fighting ended, it would be better known as the "River of Death."

The Battle of Chickamauga began with confusion. Rosecrans thwarted an attempted surprise attack by the Confederates, but he'd failed to realize how many soldiers the Confederates had

Go On

sent into the fight. The Confederates had about 66,000 soldiers to the Union's 57,000. More and more segments of the two giant armies began fighting at Chickamauga until both became completely mired in combat.

General Bragg and the Confederate army were on the offensive, aggressively attacking Union positions. The Union troops, on the other hand, took the defensive. They carefully reorganized their ranks, and some even used felled trees to build breastworks, or protective fences. The Confederates charged these breastworks again and again, each time being <u>rebuffed</u>.

Once again, confusion reigned on the battlefield. One of Rosecrans's officers misunderstood the general's orders and moved his soldiers away from the rest of the army. This left a part of the Union position undefended. When this happened, General James Longstreet led Confederate soldiers against the undefended breastworks.

Longstreet's attack finally broke through the Union forces, which began to retreat. One by one, the segments of the Union army withdrew to the north, toward Tennessee. Confederates raced forward to shoot down the fleeing soldiers.

Only one Union group remained in Chickamauga. This was a small unit led by Major General George Thomas. Thomas bravely defended his position against Longstreet's multiple attacks, thus earning the nickname "The Rock of Chickamauga." Although Thomas was eventually forced to retreat, his persistence helped ensure that the rest of the Union troops could get away safely.

Rosecrans moved his army back into southern Tennessee. Bragg and other Confederate leaders later surrounded Rosecrans and began a siege. The trapped Union soldiers were unable to escape, and other armies from the North had to be sent to their rescue.

The Battle of Chickamauga was one of the most horrible clashes in the Civil War. Over the battle's three days, almost 35,000 soldiers were killed or wounded. Although Confederate losses were greater, most historians consider them to have been the victors. The Confederate soldiers had stopped a potentially devastating attack on Georgia.

Both Union and Confederate troops fought bravely at Chickamauga and their courage and suffering will be long remembered.

---

39. Which pair of words from this passage is an example of alliteration?

     A. *ultimate* and *victor*
     B. *climactic* and *clashes*
     C. *killed* and *wounded*
     D. *Native* and *American*

40. As used in the passage, <u>rebuffed</u> **most** nearly means

    A. *kept nearby.*
    B. *allowed in.*
    C. *guided through.*
    D. *forced away.*

41. Which **best** describes the way in which the passage is structured?

    A. a sequence of events
    B. a problem followed by a solution
    C. argument with evidence
    D. details describing a character

42. Which assertion is **best** supported by the evidence in the passage?

    A. Confederate soldiers were always on the defensive.
    B. Knoxville was a more important city than Atlanta.
    C. Most Civil War battles occurred in southern states.
    D. William Rosecrans was the Union's best general.

43. According to this author, what was the cause of General Bragg's move to Knoxville?

    A. He believed Rosecrans would march south.
    B. He believed Rosecrans would attack Knoxville.
    C. Knoxville was not important to the Confederates.
    D. Knoxville had poor roads and jagged mountains.

44. Which of these facts from the passage would be most relevant to use in a presentation about medical needs in the Civil War?

    A. General Longstreet broke the Union defenses.
    B. Major General Thomas fought on after the retreat.
    C. Almost 35,000 soldiers were killed or wounded.
    D. Commanders planned maneuvers during the winter.

Go On

45. What is the meaning of the Native American word *Chickamauga*?

    A. *The Rock*
    B. *The Cumberland*
    C. *River of Death*
    D. *Stagnant River*

46. Suppose you are writing an essay about your grandparents' lives for a family history book. Which of the following is the best way to state your research question?

    A. How were my grandparents important to my family?
    B. When and where were my grandparents born?
    C. What did my grandparents think of one another?
    D. How did my grandparents feel about families?

47. Which of the following sentences is written correctly?

    A. Aunt Marissa said to pick up you're laundry.
    B. Aunt Marissa said, "to pick up you're laundry."
    C. Aunt Marissa said to pick up your laundry.
    D. Aunt Marissa said: to pick up your laundry.

Go On

Passage 7

Read the following poem and answer questions 48 through 54.

The Waste Land, V. What the Thunder Said

by T. S. Eliot

Thomas Stern Eliot, better known as T. S. Eliot, was one of the most influential poets of the twentieth century. His poem "The Waste Land" is considered one of the greatest literary achievements of all time.

    After the torchlight red on sweaty faces
    After the frosty silence in the gardens
    After the agony in stony places
    The shouting and the crying
5   Prison and palace and reverberation
    Of thunder of spring over distant mountains
    He who was living is now dead
    We who were living are now dying
    With a little patience
10   Here is no water but only rock
    Rock and no water and the sandy road
    The road winding above among the mountains
    Which are mountains of rock without water
    If there were water we should stop and drink
15   Amongst the rock one cannot stop or think
    Sweat is dry and feet are in the sand
    If there were only water amongst the rock
    Dead mountain mouth of carious teeth that cannot spit
    Here one can neither stand not lie nor sit
20   There is not even silence in the mountains
    But dry sterile thunder without rain
    There is not even solitude in the mountains
    But red sullen faces sneer and snarl
    From doors of mudcracked houses

Go On

48. This poem is an example of modernist poetry because of its

    A. use of free verse.
    B. use of end rhyme.
    C. focus on telling a story.
    D. focus on inner feelings.

49. As used to describe the mountain, the phrase "mouth of carious teeth that cannot spit" is an example of which literary device?

    A. personification
    B. assonance
    C. allusion
    D. simile

50. Which pair of words from the poem is an example of end rhyme?

    A. *rock* and *stop*
    B. *sweat* and *feet*
    C. *sullen* and *sneer*
    D. *faces* and *places*

51. The point of view used in the poem reveals the poet's feelings of

    A. anger.
    B. sadness.
    C. frustration.
    D. hopelessness.

52. In the poem, the images of dry, sandy places without water are metaphors for

    A. hate.
    B. grief.
    C. death.
    D. murder.

Go On

53. Which **best** describes the way in which the poem is structured?

    A. comparison and contrast
    B. details describing a place
    C. a problem followed by solutions
    D. a question followed by an answer

54. As used in the poem, the phrase "But red sullen faces sneer and snarl" is an example of which literary device?

    A. simile
    B. allusion
    C. metaphor
    D. alliteration

Go On

Passage 8

Read the following passage and answer questions 55 through 60.

Unwinding Our Minds

Sarah Stickle, Editor
Atlanta Daily News
1121 S. Washington Avenue
Atlanta, GA 30302

Dear Editor:

People today seem to be more <u>vulnerable</u> to stress than ever before. In the slow-paced world of the past, people were content to loll around after dinner, talking until the sun went down, signaling the end of the day. This world no longer exists; our days do not end at sundown, and many of us feel both societal and personal pressure to limit our leisure time.

One reason for this phenomenon is the technological advances that make it possible to contact anyone, anywhere, anytime. Work no longer ends when one leaves the office; it can continue long into the night if we allow ourselves to keep going. Research can be conducted from home without setting foot inside a library. It is harder to relax at home when we know it is possible to keep working.

Another reason we are so stressed is that our current world is filled with multitasking, both at home and at work. While women and men of the past occupied separate and distinct roles, today's men and women fill the historical tasks of both genders at once. Our busy lives cause our minds to work overtime, leading to tension, sleeplessness, and extreme fatigue. This type of behavior is bad for us.

However, not everyone has fallen into the trap of modern stressors. Many people find time to unwind through a variety of relaxation methods. Yoga provides us with a way to relax the body and mind through stretching and deep-breathing exercises. Aromatherapy allows us to learn which natural scents can calm our spirits. Visualization techniques can cause us to feel as if we are transported to a calmer time and place. If we can learn to embrace these relaxation tools as a society, we can reverse the stress that plagues us.

Sincerely,

Tyler Harris

Go On

55. Which **best** describes how this passage is structured?

    A. a chronological sequence of events
    B. a problem followed by several causes
    C. a list of the author's best characteristics
    D. a question followed by several explanations

56. The point of view in the passage reveals the author's

    A. belief that relaxation techniques benefit people.
    B. desire to abandon the pressures of modern life.
    C. stress over the problems at work and home.
    D. distaste of technological advances.

57. The author uses examples from the past in the passage in order to

    A. convince people to leave work at the office.
    B. explain why he thinks the past was better.
    C. support the idea of increased leisure time.
    D. show the reader how much has changed.

58. As used in the passage, <u>vulnerable</u> **most** nearly means

    A. *exposed.*
    B. *receptive.*
    C. *oblivious.*
    D. *welcoming.*

59. What is the **most likely** reason the author wrote this passage?

    A. to convince people that it is important to take time away from work
    B. to explain the causes of stress and offer some easy relaxation tips
    C. to compare the past to the present and explain which is better
    D. to persuade people to spend more time with their families

60. Besides the editor, for which audience is the passage intended?

    A. people who work from home
    B. people who work too much
    C. people who practice yoga
    D. people who feel stressed

Stop

Georgia High School Writing Test

Practice Test 2

For the **Georgia High School Writing Test** (GHSWT) you will be given an answer book with a prompt inside. You will respond to a prompt that asks you to persuade.

The GHSWT is administered in one two-hour session. Ninety minutes of this session are used for student writing time. You will also use this time to edit and revise your writing. Your composition for this test will be no more than two pages in length.

Your composition should be written neatly and should show that you can organize and express your thoughts clearly and completely. You may not use a dictionary or other reference materials.

Writing Prompt

Writing Situation

The mayor of your town wants to build a youth center so that students will have a safe place to spend time outside of school. His plans for the center include homework help, reading programs, counseling services, artistic guidance, and athletic recreational activities. However, the site on which he plans to build the center is an old, run-down park that is currently home to animals such as squirrels and birds. Some citizens feel that the youth center is valuable enough that the old park should be sacrificed, while others feel that it is wrong to chase animals from their homes to make room for a new building.

Directions for Writing

Write a paper to be presented at a meeting of the city council in which you describe your views on getting rid of the park to make room for the youth center. Clearly state your position. Convince the city council to agree with you by providing concrete reasons, evidence, and supporting details.

Go On

Student Writing Checklist for Persuasive Writing[1]

Prepare yourself to write:

- ☐ Read the *Writing Situation* and *Directions for Writing* carefully.
- ☐ Brainstorm for ideas.
- ☐ Consider how to address your audience.
- ☐ Decide what ideas to include and how to organize them.
- ☐ Write only in English.

Make your paper meaningful:

- ☐ Use your knowledge and/or personal experiences that are related to the topic.
- ☐ Express a clear point of view.
- ☐ Fully support your argument with specific details, examples, and convincing reasons.
- ☐ Include an appeal to logic and/or emotions.
- ☐ Present your ideas in a clear and logical order.
- ☐ Stay on topic.

Make your paper interesting to read:

- ☐ Use examples and details that would be convincing to your audience.
- ☐ Use appropriate voice that shows your interest in the topic.
- ☐ Use precise, descriptive, vivid words.
- ☐ Vary the type, structure, and length of your sentences.
- ☐ Use effective transitions.

Edit and revise your paper:

- ☐ Consider rearranging your ideas and changing words to make your paper more effective.
- ☐ Add additional information or details to make your paper complete.
- ☐ Proofread your paper for usage, punctuation, capitalization, and spelling.

---

[1]Retrieved from *http://gadoe.org/_documents/curriculum/testing/ga_writing_assessment_ghswt.pdf*.

Stop

Answers

PT1 C 2 ELAALRL1.b.nonfiction

Answer choices A, B, C, and D would be appropriate in a presentation about zoology, the study of animals. Only answer choice C also pertains to the study of human nature.

1 B 3 ELA11C1

In the sentence, the semicolon should be changed to a colon since it is introducing a list of items.

2 C 3 ELA11C1

Answer choice C uses the most formal language. All of the other choices mention inappropriate topics or use informal language.

3 B 2 ELAALRL2.poetry.a

Although the poem mentions dancing, games, and rain, the entire poem conveys the feeling of spring.

4 A 1 ELAALRL1.poetry.a.i

Alliteration is the repetition of the same consonant sound. The phrase "luscious the little lame balloonman" employs multiple *el* sounds.

5 C 1 ELAALRL1.poetry.a.ii

Ballads, sonnets, and blank verse are all types of poetry that use a certain strict form. Free verse allows for more freedom of structure and word choice, as in this poem.

6 B 2 ELAALRL3.b.v

Answer choices A, C, and D are not characteristics of the postmodern movement. Only answer choice B is a characteristic of the postmodern movement.

7 C 2 ELAALRL1.poetry.b

The tone of this poem is childlike and the subject matter is a child's view of the beginning of spring. The running together of words most likely represents the breathlessness of children as they energetically jump from one activity to the next.

8 D 2 ELAALRL1.poetry.b

Puddles are not generally considered a good thing. To describe them as wonderful is a paradox.

9 B 1 ELAALRL5.a

A misconception is a false idea that is widely held to be true.

10 A 2 ELAALRL2.a

The main idea of this article is that the body needs carbohydrates to carry out certain functions and protect against certain diseases within the body.

11 C 1 ELAALRL1.nonfiction.a

The passage asserts that carbohydrates are beneficial and then provides a list of details that serve as evidence to support this assertion.

12 A 2 ELAALRL1.nonfiction.b

The author stresses that you should eat a balanced diet and even includes an illustration of the food pyramid to reinforce this assertion.

13 B 2 ELAALRL1.nonfiction.c

The author refers to patients that come into her weight-loss clinic. This is what makes her qualified to write about carbohydrates.

14 D 1 ELAALRL5.a

In this context, the word *contracting* means *acquiring*, as in a disease.

15 B 2 ELAALRL1.nonfiction.b

The author says that many antioxidants are obtained through eating carbohydrates.

16 A 3 ELA11C1

When dealing with things that can be counted, use the word *fewer*. Only use the word *less* when describing things that cannot be counted by unit. Also, the word *let's* does have an apostrophe—it is a contraction for *let us*.

17 C 3 ELA11C1

Answer choice C uses the most formal language. All of the other choices mention inappropriate topics and use informal language.

18 B 2 ELAALR1.fiction.c

The author uses this simile to describe the thick layer of smoke hovering over the field.

19   A   1   ELAALR1.fiction.a

Tom Little smiles at George when he punches his ticket, thus showing that he doesn't have any ill will toward George. However, Tom is described as having sent thousands of Georges on their way and is eager to discuss the details of his upcoming fishing trip. He is pretty indifferent to the fact that George is leaving.

20   B   1   ELAALR1.fiction.d

George counts his money because he wants to protect it and himself so he doesn't "appear green" on his trip. His going over the advice his father gave him and taking inventory of what he's brought indicate that George is slightly nervous about his impending trip.

21   D   1   ELAARL5.a

The narrator explains that the air "vibrated with the song of insects." The use of the word *song* implies that the most likely meaning of the word *vibrated* in this context is *hummed*.

22   D   2   ELAALR2.a

Only answer choice D is a theme in the story.

23   C   1   ELAALR1.fiction.a

George's actions in his final hours definitely show that he wants to remember the small town. Also, during his departure, he doesn't daydream about his next adventure but instead about the subtle aspects of the town. This shows his sentimentality for the town. However, his actions also imply that he is excited to leave.

24   C   1   ELAALRL5.a

The author uses the word *tranquil* to describe sunny spots where students study. This would most likely be a peaceful place.

25   A   2   ELAALRL2.a

The central idea, or theme, of the passage is that Carrie changed her lifelong feelings about college.

26   D   2   ELAALRL1.nonfiction.c

The author writes about meeting Adrian's friends and notes that they were nice to her. This shows the students' friendliness.

27   B   2   ELAALRL1.nonfiction.c

The narrator is clearly excited about the decision she has made. She opens by noting how life changes quickly, and builds up to her announcement about college. She uses exclamation points to show that she's enthusiastic.

28   C   1   ELAALRL1.nonfiction.a

This diary entry is constructed mostly like a sequence of events. After a brief introduction, it explains how Adrian returned home, the discussion she had with Carrie, and then each event during Carrie's visit to the university.

29   C   2   ELAALRL1.nonfiction.b

Carrie writes that, although Adrian helped show her new ideas, the ultimate decision to choose to go to college was her (Carrie's) decision alone.

30   A   1   ELAALRL1.nonfiction.a

In commenting on how quickly life can change, the author prepares the reader for some major development or decision.

31   C   3   ELA11C1

Answer choice C is the only choice that does not include inappropriate information.

32   D   3   ELA11C1

The sentence is correct as is.

33   A   2   ELAALRL2.fiction.a

The narrator is reflecting on his own life as well as on the life of his aunt.

34   A   1   ELAALRL5.a

The narrator uses the expression when explaining that his aunt caught the attention of his uncle.

35   C   2   ELAALRL1.fiction.c

The narrator says that he regretted suggesting the concert to his aunt because she seems so preoccupied with the farm that she seems to have forgotten such things.

36   B   2   ELAALRL1.fiction.c

Hearing the music at the matinee makes Aunt Georgiana realize what she has been missing out on: her love of music.

37   B   1   ELAALRL1.fiction.a

The narrator compares the love of music to a plant that appears to be dead but comes back to life when put in water.

38   D   1   ELAALRL5.a

The word *inexplicable* means *unable to be explained*, a definition that could also be used for the word *mysterious*.

39   B   2   ELAALRL5.nonfiction.c

Alliteration occurs when words begin with similar sounds. The only words here that begin with similar sounds are *climactic* and *clashes*, which both begin with the *cl* sound.

40   D   1   ELAALRL5.a

In the passage, it says that Confederate attacks on the Union defenses were rebuffed. By looking at the context of this statement, you can tell that the attacks were forced away.

41   A   1   ELAALRL1.nonfiction.a

This passage is structured simply as a sequence of events. After a brief introduction, the author goes step-by-step through the events surrounding the battle.

42   C   2   ELAALRL1.nonfiction.b

In the passage, it says that most battles were fought in Virginia, a southern state. It also says that battles took place throughout the Southeast, and explains a battle in Georgia. This leads to the conclusion that most battles took place in the South.

43   B   2   ELAALRL1.nonfiction.b

The author writes that Bragg quickly moved to Knoxville to fortify the city against an expected attack by Rosecrans and the Union army.

44   C   2   ELAALRL1.nonfiction.b

The information about how many soldiers were killed and wounded would be most relevant to a presentation about medical needs in the war. The immense number of injuries caused in battle would require extensive medical care.

45 D 1 ELAALRL5.a

Although each of these phrases is mentioned in the text, the author explains that the original Native American meaning of *Chickamauga* is *Stagnant River*.

46 A 3 ELA11C1

Each of these questions might be of service to you if you were writing an essay about grandparents. However, the one question that would best fit a family history book is answer choice A. To make the essay fit into the book, it should address why your grandparents were important to the family's story.

47 C 3 ELA11C1

Answer choice A uses the incorrect form of *your*. Answer choice B uses the same incorrect form and also misuses quotation marks. Answer choice D places a colon where it doesn't belong. The correct sentence is answer choice C.

48 A 1 ELAALRL1.poetry.a.ii

Modernist poetry rejects formal standards of poetry such as focus on rhyme and meter. Because the poem rhymes in some places, doesn't rhyme in others, and has a very irregular meter, it can be classified as free verse, which is a characteristic of modernist literature.

49 A 1 ELAALRL1.poetry.a.iii

Mountains do not have mouths or teeth; the author is clearly using personification.

50 D 1 ELAALRL1.poetry.a.i

End rhyme occurs when words at the end of lines rhyme. The only example of this is in the two lines that end with the words *faces* and *places*.

51 D 1 ELAALRL1.poetry.a

The lack of water and the focus on death and dying suggests that the speaker feels a sense of hopelessness. There is no place for him to sit and rest and there seems to be no hope of finding refuge.

52 C 1 ELAALRL1.poetry.iii

Every living thing needs water to survive. The poem's images of dry, sandy places without water conjure up images of death.

53 B 1 ELAALRL1.poetry.a

The poem mainly uses details to describe the setting in which the speaker finds himself.

54 D 1 ELAALRL1.poetry.i

The repetition of the s sound throughout the line shows that the author is using alliteration for emphasis. The harsh sound of the s seems to imply pain and reinforce the negative imagery in the poem.

55 B 1 ELAALRL1.nonfiction.a

The author identifies a problem and then proceeds to list several factors in our society that contribute to the problem.

56 A 1 ELAALRL1.nonfiction.a

The author's point of view shows that he believes relaxation techniques are the best answer to the stress that plagues our society.

57 D 2 ELAALRL1.nonfiction.c

The author uses examples from the past in his letter to show the reader how much our society has changed. His explanations illustrate that while some of these advances have made our lives much easier, they can also contribute to stress.

58 A 1 ELAALRL5.a

Vulnerable means *at risk* or *exposed to*. The author feels that because of various factors, people today seem more exposed to stressors than were people in the past.

59 B 2 ELAALRL1.nonfiction.c

The reason the author wrote this letter is to explain what he believes to be the major causes of stress in our society and offer easy tips to help people relax.

60 D 2 ELAALRL1.nonfiction.b

The author is writing to anyone that experiences stress, which includes most people on the planet.

Writing Sample Answer

I think that a youth center would be very valuable for the children of our community. While it is unfortunate that the animals in the old park would be displaced from their homes, I think that the benefits of the youth center would solve problems in our community that are more important than the fate of a few squirrels and birds.

I agree with the mayor that a youth center would provide children with a safe place to spend time after school. I have heard many students talk about the bad things that happen in their neighborhoods. Sometimes children end up playing basketball on the same courts where the criminals in their neighborhoods play. It is hard for some children to avoid the people in these neighborhoods. Some of these children end up spending so much time with these bad people that they end up viewing them as role models. Kids are very easily influenced, and if they are not given alternatives, they will often adopt the bad behaviors of those around them. Many children who grow up to be criminals did not choose this lifestyle, but fell into it because they had no other opportunities. Providing children in these neighborhoods with a youth center will give them a better place to spend time and better role models, thereby increasing their chances for academic and personal success.

Children who do not live in these neighborhoods could greatly benefit from the youth center as well. Many children have working parents or guardians who cannot always be there when children need help with homework or personal issues. Some children get bad grades because they do not get the help that they need outside of school. Others feel that they can't talk to their parents about things that are bothering them because their parents might get upset or the children might be punished. Providing these children with homework help and counseling could allow them to work out academic and personal problems that they may not be able to solve otherwise. Also, children may get to experience new athletic and artistic activities that they don't have the chance to sample at home. Sports programs and art classes cost money. Offering these activities to children at little or no cost would allow a greater number of children to develop skills they are currently unable to cultivate.

As for the animals in the old park, they are currently the only ones who benefit from the park. No one visits the park anymore, and no one takes care of it. It may be a safe place for squirrels, but it is not a safe place for children. I think that the squirrels and birds in the old park will be able to find other places to live. There are plenty of natural areas around town where these animals can live. Maybe the city should make an effort to make sure that these animals are relocated to new natural areas. Regardless, I believe that the children of this town deserve better opportunities and chances to grow academically, personally, and artistically. This is why I think that the city should build the new youth center.

Index

A

Accommodations, xi–xii
Advertisement
    reading, 64
Aesthetic reasons, 20
"Ah, Are You Digging on My Grave" (Hardy), 116–117
Allusion, 2
"American Aid Essential for First-Rate Foreign Relations," 97
"Annabel Lee" (Poe), 10–11
Author's purpose, 52–67
    example reading passages for, 54–64
    Georgia Performance Standards
        ELAALRL1.fiction, xviii, 52
        ELAALRL1.nonfiction, xviii, 52
        ELAALRL2, xviii, 52
        ELAALRL4, xix, 53
    nonfiction, 92
    overview of questions about, 53
Author's word choice, 20–21

B

Beowulf, 111
Berrent Art Academy, 64
Bierce, Ambrose, 57–58
Biodiesel fuel, 41
Bronte, Emily, 6

C

Chameleons, 28–29
Chopin, Kate, 71
Cognates, 1–2
Composition, 121–135
    content and organization, 124–125
    criteria for effective persuasive writing, 123–124
    developing, 124
    drafting, 124
    Georgia Performance Standards
        ELAALRC3, xxii, 121
        ELAALRC4, xxii, 121
        ELA11C1, xxii, 121
        ELA11C2, xxiii, 122
    grading, 125–127
        conventions, 127
        ideas, 126
        organization, 126
        style, 127
    mechanics, 125
    prewriting, 124
    revision, 124, 130–134
    sample top-scoring composition, 129–130
    sentence formation, 125
    student writing checklist for persuasive writing, 128
    usage, 125
    writing prompts, 122, 129
Content, of composition, 124–125
Context, historical, 70
Context clues, 2
Conventions
    composition grading, 127
Crop circles, 93–95
"Curious Crop Circles," 93–95

D

"Daydreams Save the Day" (Sanchez), 102–103
Diaries, 91
"Don't Sweat Global Warming," 54–56
Drafting stage, 124
Driving age, 99–100

E

Education, year-round, 60–62
Essays, 91. *See also* Composition
Evidence, 91

F

"False Gems, The" (Maupassant), 76–80
Fiction, 68–89
    elements of American fiction, 70
    example reading passages for, 71–86
    Georgia Performance Standards
        ELAALRL1.fiction, xix, 68
        ELAALRL2, xix–xx, 68–69
        ELAALRL3, xx, 69
    historical context, 70
    interpretation, 70
    theme, 70
Figurative language
    poetry, 107, 108
"Fuel of the Future" (Greene), 41

G

Georgia High School Graduation Test (GHSGT)
  additional information and support, xiii
  format of, xiii
  registration fee, xi
  study tips for, xiii
  test accommodations and special situations, xi–xii
  test-taking strategies, xiv–xv
  types of passages in, xiv
  uses of, x
  waiver and variance, xi–xii
  when and where given, xi
  who takes test, x
Georgia High School Writing Test (GHSWT). *See also* Composition
  additional information and support, xiii
  criteria for effective persuasive writing, 123–124
  format of, xiii
  registration fee, xi
  study tips for, xiii
  test accommodations and special situations, xi–xii
  test-taking strategies, xiv–xv
  uses of, x
  waiver and variance, xi–xii
  when and where given, xi
  who takes test, x
Georgia Performance Standards
  author's purpose
    ELAALRL1.fiction, xviii, 52
    ELAALRL1.nonfiction, xviii, 52
    ELAALRL2, xviii, 52
    ELAALRL4, xix, 53
  composition
    ELAALRC3, xxii, 121
    ELAALRC4, xxii, 121
    ELA11C1, xxii, 121
    ELA11C2, xxiii, 122
  fiction
    ELAALRL1.fiction, xix, 68
    ELAALRL2, xix–xx, 68–69
    ELAALRL3, xx, 69
  main idea and theme
    ELAALRL1.fiction, xvii, 36
    ELAALRL2, xvii–xviii, 36
  nonfiction
    ELAALRL1.nonfiction, xxi, 90
  poetry
    ELAALRL1.poetry, xxi, 107
  vocabulary
    ELAALRL1.fiction, xvi, 19
    ELAALRL1.nonfiction, xvi, 19
    ELAALRL1.poetry, xvii, 20
    ELAALRL5, xvi, 1

"Georgia's Right Whales," 8
Gilman, Charlotte Perkins, 38–39
Global warming, 54–56
Golden, Eliot, 99–100
Grading composition, 125–127
Greene, Shelby, 41
Greenhouse gases, 54–56

H

Hardy, Thomas, 23, 116–117
"Hypnotist, The" (Bierce), 57–58

I

Ideas
  composition grading, 126
Idioms, 1
Iroquois people, 13–15
"I Wandered Lonely As a Cloud" (Wordsworth), 113–114

J

Journals, 91

L

Letters, 91
"Lively Lizards," 28–29
Lizards, 28–29
"Logan's Lesson," 43–45
Logic, 91
"London Thoroughfare. 2 A.M., A" (Lowell), 109–110
Lowell, Amy, 109–110

M

Main idea and theme, 36–51
  example reading passages for, 38–48
  fiction and, 70
  Georgia Performance Standards
    ELAALRL2, xvii–xviii, 36
    ELAALRL1.fiction, xvii, 36
  identifying main idea, 37
  identifying theme, 37
"Man He Killed, The" (Hardy), 23
Maupassant, Guy de, 76–80
Mechanics, 125
Mood, 21–22

N

Nonfiction, 90–106
   author's purpose, 92
   evidence and logic, 91
   example reading passages for, 93–103
   Georgia Performance Standards
      ELAALRL1.nonfiction, xxi, 90
   language use, 92
   major varieties of, 90–91
   rhetorical strategies, 92
   style, 92
   syntax, 92
Northern right whales, 8

O

Organization
   composition grading, 126
Organization, of composition, 124–125

P

Performance Standards. *See* Georgia Performance
      Standards
Persuasive writing. *See also* Composition
   criteria for effective, 123–124
   student writing checklist for, 128
Poe, Edgar Allan, 10–11
Poetry, 107–120
   elements of, 108
   example reading passages for, 109–117
   figurative language, 107, 108
   form, 107, 108
   Georgia Performance Standards
      ELAALRL1.poetry, xxi, 107
   sound, 107, 108
Prefix, 3–4
Prewriting stage, 124

R

Ray, Jacqueline, 47–48
Reading passages
   author's purpose, 54–64
   fiction, 71–86
   main idea and theme, 38–48
   nonfiction, 93–103
   overview of types of, xiv
   poetry, 109–117
   vocabulary, 6–15, 23–32
Reference material, 3
Reich Sidney, 47–48
Revision, 124, 130–134

Rhetorical reasons, 20
Rhetorical strategies
   nonfiction, 92
Right whales, 8
"Ripe Figs" (Chopin), 71
Root word, 3

S

"Safe at Sixteen? Why We Should Raise the Legal
      Driving Age" Golden, 99–100
Sanchez, Ricardo, 102–103
Sentence formation, 125
Shakespeare, William
   biographical information, 31–32
Simonson, Rebecca, 60–62
Six Nations, 13–15
"Six Nations of the Iroquois, The," 13–15
Sound, poetry, 107, 108
Speeches, 91
Spiders, 47–48
Standards. *See* Georgia Performance Standards
Style
   composition grading, 127
   nonfiction, 92
Suffix, 3, 5
"Superstition Mission, A," 25–26
Syntax, 20–21
   nonfiction, 92

T

Tarantulas, 47–48
"Tarantula Tamer" (Ray), 47–48
Theme. *See* Main idea and theme
"Thinking Spot, The," 73–74
Tone, 21–22
"Truth about Year-Round Education, The"
      (Simonson), 60–62
"Twins," 82–86

U

Usage, 125

V

Variance, xii
Vocabulary, 1–35
   allusion, 2
   author's word choice, 20–21
   cognates, 1–2
   context clues, 2
   example reading passages for, 6–15, 23–32

foreign word, 3
Georgia Performance Standards
    ELAALRL5, xvi, 1
    ELAALRL1.fiction, xvi, 19
    ELAALRL1.nonfiction, xvi, 19
    ELAALRL1.poetry, xvii, 20
idioms, 1
prefix, 3–4
reference material, 3
rhetorical and aesthetic choices, 20
suffix, 3, 5
syntax, 20–21
tone and mood, 21–22
word structure, 3–5
words with multiple meanings, 1–2

W

Waiver, xi–xii
Whales, 8
Word structure, 3–5
Wordsworth, William, 113–114
Writing. *See* Composition
Writing prompts
    sample, 129
    types of, 122
Wuthering Heights (Brontë), 6

Y

Year-round education, 60–62
"Yellow Wallpaper, The" (Gilman), 38–39

Image Credits

"The Six Nations of the Iroquois" (p. 13) courtesy New York Public Library.

"Superstition Mission" (p. 25) by ©iStockphoto.com/Jaimie D. Travis

"Tarantula Tamer" (p. 47) by ©iStockphoto.com/David Haynes.

"The Thinking Spot" (p. 73) by ©iStockphoto.com/Jan Ball.

"Excerpt from 'The False Gems'" (p. 76) by ©iStockphoto.com/Rasmus Rasmussen.

"Twins" (p. 83) by ©iStockphoto.com/Mandy Godbehear.

"Curious Crop Circles (p. 93) by ©iStockphoto.com/George Cairns.

"Safe at Sixteen" (p. 99) by ©iStockphoto.com/Cole Vineyard.

"Daydreams Save the Day" (p. 103) by ©iStockphoto.com/Amanda Rohde.

Daffodils image (p. 113) by ©iStockphoto.com/Bill Storage.

"Majestic Redwoods" (p. 138) by ©iStockphoto.com/Benek Lisefski.

"All About the Music" (p. 154) by ©iStockphoto.com/Galina Barskaya.

"The Coolest Invention" (p. 161) courtesy Carrier Corporation.

"Bird Brains" (p. 182) by ©iStockphoto.com/Lee Feldstein.

"College-Bound Turnaround" (p. 193) by ©iStockphoto.com/Jason Stitt.

NOTES